New Library of Pastoral Care
GENERAL EDITOR: DEREK BLOWS

Learning to Care

New Library of Pastoral Care
GENERAL EDITOR: DEREK BLOWS

———

LEARNING TO CARE

Christian Reflection on Pastoral Practice

———

Michael H. Taylor

First published 1983
Third impression 1987
SPCK
Holy Trinity Church
Marylebone Road
London NW1 4DU

Acknowledgement
The extract from 'Four Quartets' by T. S. Eliot
is reprinted by permission of Faber and Faber Ltd.

British Library Cataloguing in Publication Data

Taylor, Michael H.
   Learning to care. — (New library of pastoral care)
   1. Christian life
   I. Title   II. Series
   248.4   BV45104.A1

ISBN 0 281 04041 9

Filmset by Pioneer
Printed and bound in Great Britain by
Anchor Brendon Ltd, Tiptree, Essex

Contents

Foreword

The *New Library of Pastoral Care* has been planned to meet the needs of those people concerned with pastoral care, whether clergy or lay, who seek to improve their knowledge and skills in this field. Equally, it is hoped that it may prove useful to those secular helpers who may wish to understand the role of the pastor.

Pastoral care in every age has drawn from contemporary secular knowledge to inform its understanding of man and his various needs and of the ways in which these needs might be met. Today it is perhaps the secular helping professions of social work, counselling and psychotherapy, and community development which have particular contributions to make to the pastor in his work. Such knowledge does not stand still, and pastors would have a struggle to keep up with the endless tide of new developments which pour out from these and other disciplines, and to sort out which ideas and practices might be relevant to his particular pastoral needs. Among present-day ideas, for instance, of particular value might be an understanding of the social context of the pastoral task, the dynamics of the helping relationship, the attitudes and skills as well as factual knowledge which might make for effective pastoral intervention, and perhaps most significant of all, the study of particular cases, whether through verbatim reports of interviews or general case presentation. The discovery of ways of learning from what one is doing is becoming increasingly important.

There is always a danger that a pastor who drinks deeply at the well of a secular discipline may lose his grasp of his own pastoral identity and become 'just another' social worker or counsellor. It in no way detracts from the value of these professions to assert that the role and task of the pastor are quite unique among the helping professions and deserve to be clarified and strengthened rather than weakened. The theological commitment of the pastor and the appropriate use of his role will be a recurrent theme of the series. At the same time the pastor cannot afford to work in a vacuum. He needs to be able to communicate and co-operate with those helpers in other disciplines whose work may overlap, without loss of his own unique role. This in turn will mean being able to communicate with them through some understanding of their concepts and language.

Finally, there is a rich variety of styles and approaches in pastoral work within the various religious traditions. No attempt will be made to secure a uniform approach. The Library will contain the variety, and even perhaps occasional eccentricity, which such a title suggests. Some books will be more specifically theological and others more concerned with particular areas of need or practice. It is hoped that all of them will have a usefulness that will reach right across the boundaries of religious denomination.

DEREK BLOWS
Series Editor

Preface

Each year I enjoy working with a group of ordinands on what we have called the 'practice of theology' though it might better be called 'reflection on practice'—the central concern of this book. I have enjoyed myself even more, as I think they have, when we have been joined from time to time by lay people, students on placement and ministers working with congregations in the area. Our discussion and experiments have then been rooted in the untidiness and lively detail of everyday life and blessed with an immediacy and sense of purpose which it is not always easy for training classes to achieve. More important still, they have been immeasurably enriched by the wider range of gifts and experience and insight which we have been able to share. I have had those groups and their churches and tasks as Christians very much in mind as I have been writing and I wish to acknowledge my debt to their friendly and interested co-operation. It may be unfair to them to describe the result as a corporate effort, but I hope it does nothing to detract from our shared experience of the heart of theology as a corporate enterprise.

Because of this background I set out to write in a non-technical way, by which I mean a way that would not be unduly off-putting for those who have come to regard theology as one professional pursuit amongst others carried out by a fairly restricted circle of people to which they do not belong. I have not always succeeded, partly because of what seem to me to be the in-built intricacies of the subject, and partly because I have needed to refer to other writers, some of them very professional, for specific illustrations of what I wanted to say. This is particularly true of the central parts of the book, but I hope that even those are reasonably clear and straightforward, and I have tried in the final chapter to summarize my practical conclusions and indicate how they relate to the different stages of the preceding argument.

I confess to a certain diffidence. I want to talk about reflecting on practice and I don't. I want to talk about it because I believe it is of considerable importance for the healthy life of the Church. I don't want to talk about it because my efforts to sort out what it means to reflect theologically on our Christian obedience and how it can be done do not bring mounting satisfaction, at least not without mounting perplexity. My hope is that by putting down some rather unsatisfactory conclusions I shall encourage others to take up the issue and help me and my lay and ministerial colleagues to do better.

Talking of ministers, I will refrain from the by now standard declaration that all apparent references to men which, on examination, turn out to be unpardonably chauvinistic, in fact refer to women as well! Instead I will apologize for being too lazy or unperceptive or lacking in linguistic inventiveness to purge my material of that particular error.

I have thanked my fellow students. I should also like to thank those other colleagues who have given me time and space to do this piece of work; a number of friends, especially Frank Wright, for encouragement and good advice; and Pam Crowther for typing the manuscript.

MICHAEL H. TAYLOR

ONE

Pastoral Care and Christian Faith

My chief concern is with the 'and', not primarily with a systematic account of pastoral care or an exposition of Christian faith but with a meeting point between the two. I can best explain it in a preliminary way by referring to the world I know best.

For a number of years I have worked in theological education, mainly but not exclusively in ministerial training. The vocabulary of that world implies that 'theology' is very important. A candidate for the ministry is expected to spend several years associated with a 'theological college' or course and invariably takes a degree or diploma in 'theology' as part of basic training. In my experience ordinands are often referred to as 'theological students'. Theology appears to be central. It colours the identity of institutions and their clients and determines the content of most of what they do. Its position is stoutly defended against the onward march of practical courses.

Once this world is left behind, however, what has been central rapidly becomes marginal for many people and little attempt is made to hide the fact. A few continue to read the journals and the latest books but most find little time for any of them. The pressures are far too great. There are services and sermons to prepare, parishes and congregations to organize, rites of passage to conduct, more than a fair share of meetings and committees to attend, and the endless visiting and counselling that pastoral care requires. This busy-ness may be deplored by sophisticated observers of the ministerial life-style but it remains a fact, and one of its casualties is the theology which once seemed so very important. The books are returned to the shelves and without too much regret since it is hard to see how they can contribute to the job in hand apart from a few for immediate consumption, quickly read and immediately put to good use in sermons and discussion groups.

Besides this neglect there are signs of a failure to integrate theology with faith and practice. No one can object when there are differences of opinion between what is taught in a course of theology and what ministers believe and do, only when what is taught is not even taken into account. The familiar disturbance often experienced by students in the early stages of training when they fear that much of their faith is being undermined and taken away is a welcome sign that theology is making a difference; but there is a good deal of evidence that it is not. I think of sermons which owe nothing to the critical study of the Bible and the hesitations as well as the enrichment which it brings; of decisions taken in the local church, under the leadership of ministers, for purely practical and economic reasons or because of immediate institutional pressures, but not arising out of wider and deeper considerations about the Church's missionary task; of the contradiction between wide agreement over a participatory or collaborative church and lonely, authoritarian styles of ministry; of people who accept that God does not intervene or interfere, but who pray, and encourage others to pray, for what can only be described as old-fashioned miracles; of much talk about a Church for the poor from those whose way of life is anything but impoverished and not even a source of mild embarrassment.

If there is but a measure of truth in all this, then the huge investments of time, money and effort ploughed by the Churches into theological education and ministerial training could be going to waste. The appropriate response from theological educators like myself is not to criticize clergy and ministers for not reading enough or chide them for their inconsistencies but to try to put our own theological houses in order.

My own efforts have been on a narrow front. They do not come within shouting distance of tackling the multitude of reasons why we lack integrity and say one thing but do another, but they have been designed to bring two worlds which tend to remain far apart—the books on the shelf and the commitments in the diary—somewhat closer together. I would not claim they were novel only that I have persevered in pursuing them.

I have tried first of all to demonstrate that all the talking done by theology is of practical importance, struggling with and commenting on the meaning of human experience in this world and not merely preoccupied with another world, theoretical and remote. Second, I have shared in developing patterns of ministerial training which refuse to allow people to take traditional courses in theology and only later practise ministry either as part of their initial period of theological education or after it has been completed. Instead, theological studies of the more traditional kind and the supervised practice of ministry go hand in hand in fairly equal proportions from the start. Very often this has meant students using local congregations and communities rather than the theological college as their main residential and training base. Such arrangements at least suggest that two major areas of preparation for ministry—theology and practice—have something to do with each other, but more important, we are put in a better position to make connections between them. Many are made unselfconsciously, but a third part of the strategy is to make some of them quite deliberately, encouraging one another to engage in what is sometimes called 'doing theology' or 'putting theology to work'[1] or what I prefer to call 'the practice of Christian reflection'. Week by week, for example, students present careful reports on their practice of ministry, what they have done and what they have experienced in doing it. Just like verbatim reports in clinical pastoral training these become the raw material for evaluating people's work and discerning training needs but also for an engagement between the issues that have arisen in the practical sphere and the material they are becoming familiar with when studying the Bible, the history of the Church, the philosophy of religion, historical and systematic theology and Christian ethics. These weekly encounters are undergirded by a more systematic attempt to explain and explore how this theological reflection on practice might best be done, developing workable disciplines and procedures. Whether pursued systematically or informally the concern is with the 'and' which links the practice of ministry and Christian theology or faith.

It could be argued that the vocabulary of pastoral care, like that of ministerial training, also shows considerable respect for theology since its pastoral imagery is deeply rooted in the

Christian tradition and the world of the Bible. It does not choose to think of itself as simply 'care' but of care that is thoroughly influenced and infected by what Christianity has to say. If so it is hardly in dispute that, in recent years at least, it has been informed not by theological insights but by the theories and techniques of psychology, psychiatry and psychotherapy. Whatever other links may exist between pastoral care and Christian faith, and we shall note some of them in chapter 2, at this point they appear to be weak. A not dissimilar threefold response may be called for: changing the reputation of much theological talk; putting different worlds of discourse side by side; and at the level of conscious reflection working out how theology can make its contribution. In what follows we shall try to do all three.

As soon as we do however we are confronted with a new set of problems. Let us be content for the moment to say that when Christian faith, out of all the forms it can take, takes the form of theology, it is expressing itself in carefully chosen words. At its simplest our concern is that those who practise pastoral care, like those who practise ministry, should hear those words and take them into account. But there are at least three sources of considerable complexity. First, there are a great many words and a great many voices talking about all kinds of subjects, for although theology is strictly speaking talk about God it rapidly becomes talk about God as he is related to everything else. These voices come from different periods of history and different parts of the world; they speak in different languages and do not always agree with one another. How is it possible to hear them all, let alone bear in mind what they have to say? Second, it quickly becomes apparent that it is not simply a matter of listening to other people talking. Soon we find ourselves asking questions such as: 'Did they really say that?' and 'What did they mean?' especially when issues are in dispute. Answering these questions involves careful historical research and the critical study of texts and trying to find out the exact circumstances in which words were spoken, since the same words in different settings can have quite different meanings. These questions about what exactly was said become especially urgent when we are trying to listen to someone like Jesus of Nazareth whose teaching we regard as of supreme importance. The third source of complications has to do with establishing what might be called procedural rules for the conversation between those who practise care and all the voices which speak to them. Who will speak first? Who will set the agenda? Which voices will be allowed to have their say on this occasion? How much notice should be taken of them? Who will settle disputes and have the last word? How are these Christian words to be compared with all the other advice and information we are offered from secular sources?

Complications such as these make life difficult for anyone trying to integrate theology and practice by engaging in theological reflection and encouraging others to do the same. They are an open invitation to abandon the attempt, in which case the last state is almost certainly worse than the first. Having tried to make use of their theology it is now clear to those who previously neglected it that they were entirely justified in doing so, since the effort to put matters right turns out to be more trouble than it is worth. The practice of theological reflection is too complicated to be practical. The situation is aggravated further if we insist that most areas of Christian practice, including pastoral care, are not the preserve of ministers and clergy but the shared responsibility of the laity or all the people of God. If theology is important then it is important for them as well. If laity are to practise pastoral care then laity are to practise theological reflection; but they are likely to have even less patience with bewildering and time-consuming complications than ministers and clergy, rightly insisting that they have better things to do.

We are left challenged to make some suggestions about the 'and': the particular meeting point we have described between pastoral care (or any area of Christian obedience) and Christian faith avoiding two pitfalls. First, the business of reflection on practice must not be made so difficult and complicated that, daunted by the prospect, no one apart from a few specialists will engage in it. Second, it must be made accessible, or the whole exercise is pointless, but not in such a way as to overlook or falsely simplify the complexity which is undoubtedly there. We are looking for methods of putting theology to work which are realistic but also have integrity.

The following chapters pursue the concern I have been trying to explain. In chapter 2 I define what I mean by pastoral care. Important as it is in its own right this book is not about pastoral care as such. I do not attempt to draw conclusions about it and it is not a subject in which I have any particular expertise. It provides us here with a very necessary field of practical Christian endeavour without reference to which any discussion of reflection on practice can hardly hold up its head or make much sense. Pastoral care is not merely being 'used', however, since one of our basic premises is that if we can discover how to bring theology and practice together our practice, not to mention our theology, will gain from the encounter.

Chapter 3 asks what could be meant by 'Christian' pastoral care. Out of all the caring that is done, to which can this adjective be applied? I make the suggestion that it is not the caring which has got it right but the caring which, whether judged right or misplaced in the end, draws on the resources of Christianity, whatever it then makes of them. There are many kinds of resources to choose from, but when it comes to reflection on practice, the meeting point with which we are especially concerned, it will mean drawing on the theological resources of Christian faith.

Before discussing what those resources are and how they might be used, in chapter 4, we stop to remind ourselves that even when reflecting on practice we shall need to draw on many other resources besides Christian ones and that although they should not crowd out theology, as some have tended to do in pastoral care and counselling, they often have just as much and more that is of relevance to say.

Chapter 5 looks at one of the chief theological resources for reflection, namely Christian doctrine, and suggests that far from indulging in idle theory or otherwordly speculation doctrines are almost always talking about the practical world we live in and care for. And they do not have to talk to themselves. They can engage others in conversation. They speak the same language as the scientist or psychologist, for example, even when they have different things to say. There is common ground on which to meet and we can set about establishing some of the procedural rules for meetings.

Chapter 6 discusses a way of simplifying and handling the mass of doctrinal material by creating interpretative frameworks or telling stories.

When we turn to 'Pastoral Theology', the phrase sounds like a name for the meeting point between pastoral care and Christian theology which is our chief concern, but like 'pastoral care' it has several meanings. In chapter 7 these are noted and one of them, where a 'theology' of pastoral care means a 'theory' of pastoral care, is singled out as offering a realistic way of constantly integrating faith and practice at the level of reflection.

Another major theological resource for reflection is Jesus himself. Chapter 8 tries to face up to the immense problems which surround the Christian instinct to do as Jesus did and the attempt to test out everything that is said and done against what we know of his earthly ministry. The problems may be insuperable and one half of me frankly admits that that is so; the other half believes that following Jesus can still be a viable and creative discipline.

In a final chapter we shall acknowledge that although we may have arrived at some relatively straightforward ways of putting our theology to work, on most occasions we shall not have time to use them. We shall have to act spontaneously and in that sense 'unthinkingly'. Even when there is time to use them, these relatively straightforward ways of putting theology to work must be called into question should we neglect the complexities which lie beneath the surface. Is there then a way of organizing the life of the Church and especially of the local congregation so that by virtue of the fact that we share in it there is some hope of being formed for pastoral care even when we cannot reflect on it, and of keeping the complexities in sight without being overwhelmed by them?

Two further introductory remarks. First, having read a good many of them, it seems to me there can be little excuse for adding to the large number of books on pastoral care and counselling, even less for thinking I can add much to the few rather good ones. One that comes to mind is Alastair Campbell's *Rediscovering Pastoral Care.*[2] In it he too is concerned with the meeting point between pastoral care and theology: 'to restore to pastoral care a sense of indebtedness to *theological* insights, in an attempt to counterbalance the over-reliance in contemporary literature on the theories and terminology of psychology and psychotherapy.'[3] The method he adopts does not make unrealistic demands on would-be theologians. Concentrating on the pastoral relationship he makes use of a number of images such as shepherding, healing through wounds, wise folly, gracefulness and companionship—some more obviously rooted in the Christian tradition than others—to rekindle imaginations and 'stimulate fruitful associations of ideas' and 'convey an intuitive understanding of the care which is required of us in pastoral relationships'. All of which seems admirable. I can only hope that my discussion will complement at one or two points what he has said so well. For example Campbell has admittedly been selective. He has chosen five images out of all the illuminating things that might be said. How can we make reasonably sure that we have taken Christian insights comprehensively into account? Or again, Campbell has made clear that the pastoral relationship is characterized by mutuality. It is not a matter of expert guidance or the strong helping the weak. One person cannot find the way for another. But how in their companionship do people tackle the questions they must raise together, if not on one another's behalf, about their goals and how they are to be achieved? Yet again, the connections between theology and pastoral care, suggests Campbell, are to be made intuitively, imaginatively and by the association of ideas. On what basis do we select and justify these images? How do we keep them in mind? And what routine safety nets do we fall back on when imagination fails or we are dealing with unimaginative people like ourselves who find it difficult to make connections?

Finally, in a good-natured exchange a close relative recently described himself to me as 'an ignorant layman'. He felt left out of what he thought of as my theological world and that, whether his fault or not, it ought not to be so. Ignorance was not apparently bliss. It was easy enough to reply that when it comes to his professional world I too feel like 'an ignorant layman', but the parallel is not quite exact. Theology is faith expressing itself in words and carefully articulating its insights. If that faith is to inform the care we are all called to show for one another, then there is a degree of exclusion, of feeling left out, which is unacceptable. The world of theology is the heritage of every practising Christian. This book has been written therefore with that 'ignorant layman' very much in mind. If he reads it I hope he finds it readable, but whether he reads it or not I hope it will contribute to developing patterns of congregational life which enable him to make practical use of the theological resources of Christianity.

Having encouraged all the Lord's people to be theologians, does that rule out a sensible division of labour? I should hate to think so, and as one involved in ministerial training I shall want to ask about the special contribution which ministers and clergy can make. But the goal must be to enable lay people to do theology and reflect on their obedience whilst leaving them free for the even more important task of getting on in the everyday world with those very responsibilities they reflect about in the light of their Christian faith.

Notes

1. By David Jenkins for example; see Derek Winter, ed., *Putting Theology to Work* (CFWM 1980), p. 86.
2. Darton, Longman & Todd 1981.
3. ibid., p. 98.

TWO

What is Pastoral Care?

'Pastoral care' is a familiar enough phrase but not all that easy to define. A glance at the literature on the subject suggests it has meant different things to different people. There is nothing wrong with that; indeed the richness which comes with variety is a positive advantage provided we don't confuse matters by assuming that everyone who uses the phrase is talking about the same thing. A few short stories may be the best start to defining our own terms.

John has a colleague Martin whose career prospects do not seem to him to be bright. This is not because Martin is bad at his job or, in his late twenties, without the talents which in other circumstances might well win him promotion. The fact is that Martin is an enthusiastic and highly committed full-time employee of the Church. He works with a team in one of the departments based on the headquarters of his comparatively small denomination. He was appointed soon after student days when his gifts and his degree made him admirably suitable for the post. And the post looked like a good opportunity at the time to a young man who was not afraid to admit that he wanted to get on. Unfortunately for Martin the Church he works for has large numbers of ordained ministers on the payroll, working in local congregations and making up the majority of its headquarters staff. It has very few lay people and Martin is one of them. John, a minister, remembers another who, some years before, found in mid-career that his Church had no further paid work for him to do and that by then it was too late to look elsewhere for anything that really made use of his talents. He ended up in a job which seemed to waste them. John does not want to see the same thing happening all over again, this time to Martin; but Martin, young and idealistic, tends to think that if he does what he believes to be the right thing now then the future will take care of itself.

Peter has been a friend, though not a particularly close one, of David's since college days. They were students together in the same hostel at university though taking different courses. David was brought up in the Church and has remained an active member. Peter was never against it and had long and thoughtful conversations with David about religion but he has never been a churchgoer and would not think of himself as a Christian. Peter married Kate, a girl he also met at university and another friend of David's. Soon afterwards they moved into a house convenient for Peter's work which they shared with two others, male friends from student days. Kate couldn't get a job at first though she had qualified as a teacher. She felt a bit out of things. Peter had his work during the day and in the evenings he seemed to spend a lot of time with his two male friends. She would be included but had very little time with Peter to herself. Then she did get a job in a nearby town and began to have a life of her own with friends of her own. She often stayed out quite late enjoying their company. Peter happens to meet David whilst revisiting old haunts. It soon becomes clear from the conversation that he is afraid of losing a girl he very much loves and he appears to be looking to David for help.

Shirley is in her late forties. She lost her husband last year after a distressing illness. She has two fairly young boys barely into their early teens. Her closest friends at the church which the family attends, one boy very unwillingly, are well aware of Shirley's anxieties. Her sister was left in a similar situation some years before and she has watched the losing battle she fought bringing up her family single-handed. She is afraid the same could happen to her. On top of that her health is poor and not just since her husband died. She has been in and out of hospital and may have to undergo more tests soon. She has commented on more than one occasion that she wonders what on earth will happen to the children and only hopes she will live long enough to see them safely off her hands. Shirley doesn't make life any easier for herself by her determination to keep up appearances. She wants the family to go on living at the same standard as when her husband was alive and earning good money. So she has stayed on in a house that is bigger than they need and tries to cope with bills that are more than she can really afford.

Those who don't know her well think she is coping marvellously.

Bill is a medical student. Although he enjoys the company of women he finds he is physically attracted to men. In one case the attraction is so strong that he can only describe it as falling in love. He has not dared to so far but he would certainly like to express what he feels in a physical way. He tells the chaplain at the university church that he is ashamed of the way he feels and recent experiences haven't helped. Not long ago he came under the influence of a group of Christians with very definite views about the Bible. He admired them and joined them. In the course of one of their Bible study sessions they had read and talked about a passage in the New Testament which said that homosexuals would never get into the Kingdom of God. They of course didn't know much about Bill, but they did seem to know a lot about some other students who felt as Bill did and behaved as Bill would like to have done, and there was no hesitation in condemning them out of hand. What made the situation worse was that Bill had heard only that very day in a lecture that there were probably quite a lot of homosexuals about who couldn't stop being attracted to other men or wanting to make love to them, even if they tried.

Joseph's parents came to England from the West Indies long before he was born. He grew up in the inner city and worked until he was forty-two in a factory recently closed due to the recession. He has joined the ranks of the unemployed, which only aggravates the feeling he already had of not really being wanted in this society. Even when he had a job he picked up hints that West Indians were not very reliable workers, now he thinks people definitely regard him as work-shy. The other blacks at church know how he feels. Gordon, a white professional in the same congregation seems friendly and sympathetic but Joseph can't imagine that he understands. What worries Joseph most is what is happening to his own teenage son Daniel. He's already been in the hands of the police. He left school with three 'O' levels and a CSE but never got a job and has little prospect of getting one. Joseph has been hard on him and even used the belt on him not so many moons ago, but secretly fears Daniel is right when he says in so many words that all he'll ever get out of this rotten country is what he takes.

Phyllis is getting old and disabled. She did not marry, has never had much money, lives alone in a small terraced house and relies on her pension and a bit of social security money for a living. Until recently she managed to get to the shops and the post office once a week. One trip ended with her handbag being snatched and with it two week's money. She can't really look after herself any more, or keep herself and her home very clean. She has no relatives and no complaints. Doris, a schoolteacher, wife and mother and leading light of the local church visits Phyllis now and again and invites her to spend Christmas Day with her family. Although Doris has children and hopes they will look after her when the time comes, Phyllis' lonely decline fills her with alarm about her own old age. She also notices that although Phyllis never had much schooling she is bright and quick-witted as if she had native intelligence which had never been made the most of. Doris wonders if it is now too late and whether she has anything to learn in middle age from Phyllis' lost opportunities.

If all these stories, of John becoming involved in the career prospects of Martin, Peter talking to David about his marriage, Shirley's close friends worrying about the anxious person behind the brave façade, the chaplain listening to Bill talking about his sexuality, of Joseph and his son, and Doris keeping an eye on Phyllis, qualify as examples of pastoral care, then one defining characteristic has been ruled out from the start. Very often it is written and talked about as if it were the preserve of ordained ministers. They are sometimes even given the title of 'pastor' as if to cement the special relationship. Now their ministry will certainly involve pastoral care, and two characters in our stories are in fact ministers: John in the first and the university chaplain in the fourth. They may even have a particular contribution to make from time to time for which they are better trained and equipped than others, but all that is far from saying that they are the only people involved. Indeed on the basis of these examples the bulk of pastoral care is carried out by lay people like David and Gordon and Doris.

That word 'lay' is worth staying with for a moment. In the Church it tends to be contrasted with 'ordained'; in the everyday world it normally refers to the 'amateur' as against the 'professional', and that suggests another defining characteristic of the pastoral care we have in mind. In a number of cases professional help will almost certainly be required at some stage. One could imagine Martin for example needing to talk to a careers' adviser and Peter and his wife to a marriage guidance counsellor. Shirley is already visiting the hospital. Bill may need a psychiatrist to help him sort himself out, or perhaps a New Testament specialist to explain to him what it does and doesn't say about homosexuals! But although the need for qualified care and advice is clearly accepted along with the recognition that where it is refused damage could be done by the well-meaning but ignorant, none of the people in our stories (with the possible exception of the university chaplain who just might have been a New Testament specialist!) would make any claim to being professionals in the field. Pastoral care then, whilst ready to call on the experts, is an area in which 'lay', non-specialist people with their concern, common sense and experience have a contribution, not to say the main contribution to make.

Another assumption which tends to be made is that pastoral care is virtually identical with counselling. In some books the two terms are interchangeable, in others 'pastoral care and counselling' appear as inseparable companions. It is obvious from our stories that there is very much more to pastoral care than that. Counselling will often come into it. The university chaplain is involved with Bill in a fairly formal counselling situation and Peter is heading for one. But the care which will be exercised by Doris when she visits her old friend, and by Gordon when he stands alongside Joseph and his son, and by Shirley's friends when they surround her with practical support, is of a different kind. And even when the talking starts as it normally has to do, it might be regarded as counselling and be all the better for sticking to a few rules of thumb about being a good listener not too ready to enthuse about what worked for you or eager to hand out advice; but little self-conscious use will be made of what we often think of as professional counselling skills. Pastoral care involves a lot of conversations, but most of them are not, technically, counselling sessions involving trained counsellors.

Pastoral care, as our six stories have described it, does seem to focus on people's problems. Martin's future is in doubt at least in John's mind. Peter's marriage has run into trouble. Shirley worries about her health and Bill about his love for other men. Joseph and Daniel are out of work with little if any hope of getting jobs and Doris is looking old age in the face and not much liking what she sees. It is not a very cheerful catalogue. This particular defining characteristic of pastoral care can hardly be denied but it needs qualifying at one or two points. Life will always be problematic wherever we dig into it so that any issue we deal with in pastoral care will touch on human weakness, our limitations and our failures, and have elements in it which we would much rather didn't exist. But our stories, arbitrary and selective as they have to be, indicate that it would be quite wrong to assume that pastoral care is always and only dealing with people when they are at their weakest and their worst. It could be argued that Martin, devoted to the Church he feels called to serve and unimpressed by John's appeals to think about his long-term future, is at his strongest and his best. There is much about Shirley which is only to be admired, with her determination to battle on if only for the sake of the kids. A comment on Bill at this stage can only beg the question about his homosexuality but any attempt to care for him may well be dealing with a fact of life rather than a fault, and be faced with an opportunity for better understanding human sexuality rather than an unfortunate case of perversity; and the uncomplaining Phyllis might better be thought of, not in negative terms, but as someone not so very different from the rest of us, who has gifts still waiting to be used and potential waiting to be realized. Pastoral care is interested in humanity in its strength as well as its unavoidable weakness.

One other assumption about pastoral care seems hard to deny on the evidence of our stories. It appears to focus its attention on individuals or small-scale situations. Can any caring remain adequate for long if limited to that? John encourages Martin to reconsider his position before it is too late and he cannot get a good job outside the Church which will have nothing to offer him in a few years' time; but shouldn't John be taking on the church authorities who perpetuate a job structure which exploits and discriminates against lay employees? David sympathizes with Peter, and a marriage guidance counsellor may at some point in the future help Peter and his wife understand what is happening to their relationship; but is anyone doing anything about a social system which, having eroded the old extended family patterns, puts enormous pressures on people's marriages and appears to ease the path to the divorce courts whilst doing little to help resolve marital problems or strengthen family life? Joseph and Daniel are obvious cases where a measure of personal support and reassurance might be appreciated but where nothing can take the place of social and political reform which will give them their fair share of work or an equal opportunity to make their responsible contribution to the well-being of the community. We have looked at only three, but all six stories indicate that the issues which confront us in pastoral care have a social dimension. Is there any justification then for this rather personal, small-scale response? Not if it becomes a substitute or an excuse for social responsibility as pastoral care so often does, and not if it helps people adjust to conditions they should not adjust to anyway. But however determined action may be on the social and political front, the structures and institutions within which people have to live as best they can are not going to be changed overnight, even though they may be more open to change than we sometimes like to think, and they are never going to be perfect. Meanwhile we cannot refuse to care for Martin and Peter and Shirley and Bill and Joseph and Daniel and Phyllis within that limited and unsatisfactory social framework even whilst we make every effort to improve it by joining hands with all the forces for good and encouraging them to do the same. If pastoral care is no substitute for social action, social action of the most committed sort does not absolve us from responding immediately to individuals however provisional that response is understood to be.

A slightly different way of guarding against this individualism which colours our stories and so much pastoral care is to remind ourselves that people like Peter and Bill and Joseph and Phyllis cannot be cared for in isolation from the rest of the human community. If they have problems they are not simply their own, and if they are to find health and happiness it will depend on others finding it as well. Society as well as Bill will have to come to terms with homosexuality if he and those like him are ever to understand it and discover its real identity. Joseph will never feel reconciled in himself until others are reconciled to the black presence in Britain, taking on the issues it raises in a positive and welcoming spirit. And only when the rest of us have learned to value old age rather than resent it will people like Phyllis have a real chance to experience hers as something other than the relentless closing of doors. We do not live by ourselves and we cannot find fulfilment except in our relations with one another.

The picture of pastoral care that has emerged so far from a slightly closer look at our stories is of a by no means exclusively clerical activity. The majority of pastors are not ordained ministers; nor are they members of caring professions. If pastoral care often has to draw on skilled specialist resources much of it lies within the competence of ordinary people. It will often involve them in counselling their friends and neighbours, again not usually in a highly technical or formal sense; but it will involve much more than that as they respond in all sorts of ways to the issues which arise in other people's lives, not only when they are weak and at their worst. Because it is an immediate response it will be made largely within existing social conditions, without in any way denying the need for those conditions to be changed.

If the word 'pastoral' does not refer for us to what is done by ordained pastors, it does perhaps carry overtones of caring which takes place at a fairly personal level where one person is relating and not merely dealing with another. To complete this catalogue of defining characteristics we should add that there are at least hints in our stories, Shirley's friends for example, that pastoral care can be exercised by groups and communities and not only by individuals; and it hardly needs saying, to put it in the most general terms, that care, whatever form it takes, springs out of genuine concern for another person's well being. These defining characteristics are not put forward as a declaration of how pastoral care ought to be understood. That would require rather more argument and justification. They are put forward in a descriptive rather than a prescriptive mood: not to dictate what ought to be the case but to uncover what I have in mind, rightly or wrongly, in the discussion which follows.

THREE

What is Christian Pastoral Care?

There is one serious omission from our description of pastoral care if we rely on the evidence of our stories. In every one of them those who care are Christians. Two, John and the university chaplain, are ministers of the Church. The rest, David, Shirley and her friends, Gordon, Joseph and Doris are members of the Church. The point is not that only Christians can exercise pastoral care. That is manifestly untrue. All of us can easily call to mind examples of men and women who care for others and have cared for us along the lines described in chapter 2; and people playing a pastoral role are easily recognisable in many of our institutions. They include personal tutors in schools and colleges, welfare officers in industry, probation officers, and social workers in hospitals. Whilst some of them see their work in Christian terms, others do not understand it as being related in any way to Christian faith, and not a few relate it quite consciously to other faiths.

Our stories are not about Christians because only Christians exercise pastoral care but because our aim is to explore what it might mean to talk about 'Christian' pastoral care rather than pastoral care in general, and to examine the relationship between pastoral care and Christian faith.

It is possible to think of that relationship in at least three ways and in so doing to suggest three answers to the questions about what is meant by 'Christian' as opposed to any other kind of pastoral care. For want of better terms we will refer to them as 'transformative', 'supportive' and 'informative'. In the first case the main contribution of Christianity is to transform a person or fundamentally change that person's life, and it is that very different person who exercises pastoral care. It is Christian simply because it is done by a Christian. The fundamental difference can be thought of as a change of heart, or conversion to Jesus Christ, or as the experience of forgiveness which releases us from selfish preoccupation with our sins and destinies and gives us the security and freedom to live for others. There is nothing particularly self-conscious about it. It is as if a calculating person had been replaced by a generous one, an inward-looking person by one who is outward-going, the love of self by the love of neighbour and of God, and this new man in Christ now cares as the person he has become. One 'natural' way of behaving has been replaced by another.

Turning to the 'supportive' and 'informative' relationships, John Cobb, an American theologian,[1] usefully highlights the difference between the two. He tends to equate pastoral care with counselling and speaks first of limited relations between counselling and theology, where faith supports the counsellor in what he is trying to do but says little to him about how it should be done, so that his counselling does not vary much from anyone else's: 'When belief in God leads to assurance that no one is beyond redemption, the pastor may here hope where other counsellors despair. But theology has little to say about the goals and methods of this kind of counselling.'[2] He then goes on to speak of a much more influential role for theology, informing as well as supporting the work of the counsellor. Believing that 'the whole of pastoral care should be theologically informed' he asks whether pastors can

> bring their faith to bear on the goals, methods and resources of counselling? Is there a type of counselling that is given distinctive shape and direction not only by the pastor's socially defined role but also by Christian understanding of God and the world?[3]

I am reminded of a similar distinction between the 'supportive' and the 'informative' made by John Macquarrie when describing the contribution of Christian faith to ethics. He did not think that Christianity added much that was new to the content of ethics. It did not inform them.

> What is distinctive in the Christian ethic is not its ultimate goals or its fundamental principles, for these are shared with all serious-minded people in whatever tradition they stand. The distinctive element is the special context within which the moral life is perceived. This special context

includes . . . the many ways in which the moral life is . . . supported by Christian faith and hope.[4]

Christian hope could presumably support pastoral care with the conviction that whatever the difficulties and setbacks all will eventually be well, a conviction inspired in the early Christians by their experience of the resurrection of Jesus from the dead. This hope will do little to enlighten Gordon, for example, as he struggles with the apparently hopeless plight of Joseph and his son, but it may help to give him enough determination to persevere in the face of overwhelming odds.

Christian talk about sin can also play a supportive role. It would be very surprising if most of the characters in our stories did not meet with a measure of disappointment in their efforts to care for their friends. One can imagine Peter's marriage breaking up in spite of everything, or Bill going to pieces, ground down between his own natural desires and the disapproval, even condemnation, of his new-found Christian colleagues, and Daniel going completely off the rails in the eyes of those whom the law favours rather more than it favours him. The natural reaction to these disappointments is to give up. An alternative response, built on the doctrine of sin, is not to be surprised. The world being what it is, these set-backs are only to be expected. Once again this teaching doesn't tell us much about what to do but it does give us a certain resilience and realism so that when the set-backs occur we are not so easily put off.

The doctrine of the Holy Spirit could be equally supportive, encouraging us to assume that God is present and active in our affairs, so that the resources and possibilities which lie in any set of circumstances are greater than the ones we recognise in ourselves and those with whom we are involved. There are more reserves than meet the eye and an energetic presence which works for and in all things with those who love God. A rather different way in which faith supports pastoral care is by supplying the motivation for it and the drive. We do what we do because of the command to love God and our neighbour, or out of gratitude for the love which God has shown to us in Christ, or because we are well aware, taught by the parable of the last judgement in Matt.28, that our response to the needs of our brothers and sisters is no light matter but has consequences for all eternity. Every moment has an everlasting or 'eschatological' (talk about the last things) dimension.

The third way of understanding the contribution of Christian faith to pastoral care and the difference which makes it 'Christian' pastoral care is not that Christianity has changed or transformed the person who cares, or that faith lends a certain amount of support. It is rather that faith actually informs caring and makes a difference to how people do it and what they do. It does so in an indirect as well as a direct way. Another reference to ethics may help to clarify the point. All of us live by moral principles or rules which suggest what we should and should not do. They actually affect our behaviour so that we never tell lies for example, or we always see to our own needs before paying that much attention to anyone else's. Such rules may affect us because at a given moment we stop to think about what to do, remember the rules and put them into practice. They have directly informed our behaviour. We tell the truth. We look after number one. But on many occasions we don't stop to think and if we nevertheless tell the truth or only look after ourselves as usual it is because such principles, absorbed from our families and friends and peer groups, have become part of our consciousness or sub-consciousness over the years. They have influenced our behaviour indirectly by forming us into the kind of people we are with the kind of standards we live by. We may therefore add to transformative, supportive and informative a 'formative' way in which Christian faith contributes to pastoral care, gradually shaping us into people who habitually care for others in a particular fashion. To this we must return towards the end of our discussion, but for the time being we shall concentrate our attention on the directly informative relationship between pastoral care and Christian faith. This in no way implies that the transformative and supportive relationships are unimportant. Quite the contrary. They will often be more important than the informative one, not least on those occasions when it will prove difficult to know what our faith is saying to us, or when we suspect that it has little to add to what has been said many times before. When we don't know how to proceed or feel we know as much or as little as we shall ever know we shall value the support rather than the advice that faith can give.

But in any case these three rather different relationships between faith and pastoral care are by no means mutually exclusive. We ourselves shall see as we proceed how Christian teaching about sin, to take only one of the many doctrines, not only supports our caring by shielding us from disappointment but informs it as well; and it would obviously be unfortunate if, say, the university chaplain to whom Bill turns in his perplexity knows all the tricks of the trade that her theology can teach her and is well armed with the most comprehensive assessment of homosexuality that the latest official reports have to offer, but is not the kind of person who, for all her faults and failings, of which she is aware, can open her heart to a fellow human being and care about him. Is there much point in being informed if she is not transformed by her faith?

That having been said, it is with the informative relationship between pastoral care and Christian faith that we are mainly concerned. This partly echoes a concern expressed by a number of writers in the field of pastoral care and counselling, that it has for too long been informed by the insights of the psychiatrist and psychotherapist and too little by the insights of Christian theology. But my concern is a little wider than that.

There is, I believe, an increasingly understood rhythm about the Christian life: a cycle rather than a circle because there is about it some sense of moving forward. It does not matter greatly at what point we break into the cycle for the purpose of this brief explanation, so we will start with commitment. Christian discipleship involves us in commitment to what we have come to believe we have to do. That may be the best understanding of obedience and integrity. Christian obedience for the characters in our stories may not in the end be any kind of conformity to instructions received from elsewhere, though it may well see no need to defy them. Obedience will mean being true to their own convictions or 'doing their truth'. If John believes he must actively discourage Martin from accepting promotion within the Church, and David believes he must tell Peter a thing or two about how to treat his wife, and the chaplain believes she must introduce

Bill to some Christians who are quite open about their homosexuality, and Doris believes she must get Phyllis to an evening class once a week next winter, then however misguided or insensitive or overdirective or even ridiculous these ideas might seem to other people, this is what these Christians must do if obedience is to mean anything. As well as being committed at this conscious level to a course of action, John and David, the chaplain and Doris are also committed at a less self-conscious level in another but not unrelated way. David amongst other things is committed to a certain view of how men should treat women; John and Doris to how people should fulfil themselves; the chaplain to a rather more accepting attitude to homosexuality than Bill has so far encountered.

The next phase in the cycle is more reflective than active. It may be provoked by our own or other people's questioning of our obedience or by both. John may become less sure about what to do or someone else may object to what he is doing. He is pulled up in his tracks. His obedience is in question. But provoked or not it will be necessary from time to time to stop and think, uncovering and re-examining the assumptions and commitments of which we are less aware and drawing on what has been learnt from experience and the new insights which obedience itself may have generated. After that, fresh commitments will have to be made in the light of any new understanding we have gained of what it is we have to do.

Discipleship then is a cycle or rhythm of action and reflection: critical reflection arising out of and leading into committed action; and it is at the reflective moments in this cycle that Christian faith has the opportunity to contribute to discipleship in an informative way. My concern is to see that it does, if it can, and to explore how it can be done not just by professional theologians or even ordained ministers of the Church but by everyone in some appropriate and practical way; for if pastoral care is not to be the spiritual preserve of clergy or specialists but a thoroughly lay activity which does not exclude the specialist's contribution, the same goes for the kind of reflection which will inform it.

The real focus of our attention then is on how to draw on Christian faith when we reflect on our Christian obedience. Pastoral care is by no means the total sum of that obedience.

Other facets of it are represented by the mission and worship of the Church, family and community life, our secular jobs and by our social and political responsibilities. All of them will involve us in the rhythm of action and reflection and in trying to inform our obedience by our faith.

When the moment for reflection comes and the caring characters in our short stories stop to think about what they are doing, three sorts of questions are likely to be raised in their minds. The first has to do with the kind of situations that now face them. What is going on? What exactly are they dealing with? Why is all this happening? David, for example, knows that all is not well between his married friends Peter and Kate but he doesn't know much else; and even when he has talked with Peter into the small hours and been to see Kate and spent time with them together he still wonders where the truth lies. It occurs to him that Peter had simply not understood how Kate felt about having to share him with his friends all the time and never having him to herself; and that during the early period of marriage when there was a lot of growing together to be done and adjustments to be made as they discovered things about each other which they didn't always like, they had grown apart instead of getting closer. He also wondered whether Kate was anxious now to assert her independence. She was not going to be an 'extra' in Peter's life, there when needed and otherwise ignored. She was going to have her own life in her own circle of friends. Maybe Kate had fallen out of love with Peter, in the sense that she no longer found him attractive or likeable, so that Peter was fooling himself by thinking she only needed time to sort herself out. She was really finding a way out without telling him directly or too soon how she felt. And then David finds himself unimpressed by any of his theories. They seem obvious things to say, predictable explanations which may do more to satisfy his need to explain than to clarify the relationship between Peter and Kate. Nevertheless it is very important that the nature of their relationship should be better understood, if not by him then by them, if appropriate and helpful responses are ever to be made.

In the very different story about Daniel, to take another example, Joseph his father and Gordon his white friend at church may both wonder in their different ways what sort of a lad they are dealing with. Is he just another victim of circumstances beyond his control? Is he a 'bad boy' as Joseph has said more than once? After all not everyone who is out of work gets into trouble. Does Joseph's outward lack of sympathy for his son only aggravate his son's low opinion of himself? And when Daniel grabs what he can get and society calls it a serious crime against property, whilst he calls it taking what belongs to him but no one will give him, who has got it right? Gordon finds that a particularly difficult one to handle.

The second sort of question has to do with aims and objectives. Here we shall have to bear in mind one of the limitations we have put on our discussion. In Daniel's case it will be obvious to many, if not to all, that the aim can be nothing less than the elimination of a social system which leaves him and thousands like him feeling they don't belong and have no useful contribution to make. But whilst that aim is being pursued and without detracting the least bit from its central importance, what in the meantime does Gordon aim to do for or with Daniel? That is the admittedly limited concern of pastoral care but it does have some merit in not allowing the fact that we will not be able to change everything to become the excuse for doing nothing. Even within this restricted field, however, it may still be necessary to distinguish between long-term and short-term aims, between what we might hope to achieve eventually and what, on reflection, we have to do next.

John for example is clearly anxious about Martin's future as a layman in the full-time pay of the Church. He's been doing his best to get Martin to share his anxiety. Perhaps that qualifies as a short-term aim; but if they get talking together about Martin's career they will have to try and take the longer view. What kind of job might be right for him? John finds himself talking about talents that must be used to the full. Martin, ambitious as he is, can't shake off the conviction that, whatever the risks, he is in the right place and is called to the service of the Church.

When Doris reflects on her visits to Phyllis, she finds she has quite a lot of questions of this second sort on her mind. What should she aim to do for Phyllis in her old age and what should she try to do with herself? Life, she feels, is slipping away from them both. Should they accept the fact that you can't do everything, or quite deliberately branch out and try something new despite the fact that Phyllis finds it a great effort to do anything and Doris has quite enough to do already? What could it mean, Doris wonders, for either of them to become the kind of woman she had it in her to be? But there are much more immediate matters to be seen to, especially since Phyllis will not be able to go on living alone for very much longer. What kind of arrangements would suit her best?

The third sort of question links the other two. If caring people raise questions about where they are now and where they ought to be going, they also ask about how to get from the one to the other. What actions are most likely to prove effective? What can we do to help? How can anyone be creative in these circumstances? The chaplain who talks to Bill about the way Bill finds himself physically attracted to other men may decide that she must help Bill to feel more positively about what he has discovered about himself, not just to accept it but to affirm it. She has still to decide how best to do it, however, in the face of the strong pressures exerted on Bill from other directions, not least by Christians whom he clearly respects and probably relies on a good deal at the moment. Shirley's friends may be clear that she must be dissuaded from driving herself unreasonably hard, putting her health even more at risk in order to maintain a style of life she cannot afford for what she refers to as the sake of the children. They have yet to see how this can be done in the face of Shirley's fierce independence, and without their actions being misunderstood and regarded as interference in her private affairs and at a time when she needs their support not their criticism.

As with any attempt to classify, we have made the picture look much neater than it really is. It will often be difficult to distinguish between the different areas referred in the three types of questions: an aim (question two) may well be to find out what is going on (question one); a helpful move (question three) may well be to establish some aims and objectives (question two again). And it will be equally difficult to deal with one question at a time or at only one stage in the reflective process. Although we might do worse than try to follow an orderly sequence, rarely if ever will people begin by establishing the truth of the matter, go on to decide their aims and objectives and finally their strategy for achieving them. At many stages, for example, the 'how' question will recur: how can we best establish the truth of the matter; how can we set about establishing aims and objectives? And it is most unlikely that the truth of a situation once it has dawned on us will not change or be seen in a new light and sooner or later need reassessing. The picture then is not a neat and tidy one, but it remains true that however often they occur and at whatever stage of reflection, caring people will be left looking for answers to questions of these three kinds: 'What are we dealing with?' 'Where should we be going?' and 'How do we get there?'

It is not our purpose to answer the questions, partly because plenty of answers are available in general terms in books on pastoral care and counselling,[5] partly because we are in no position to answer them even in the six cases described, if only for lack of information, but mainly because the focus of our attention is not the answers to questions which arise when we reflect on our Christian obedience in general and our pastoral care in particular, but how to arrive at our own answers informed by our Christian faith.

If, however, we did answer the questions there is every likelihood that we should end up with several answers to every one of them. David can give more than one account of what is going on between his friends Peter and Kate; Daniel can be seen as a victim and as a troublemaker; John thinks that Martin should change his job for his own good and Martin thinks that he should stay; Doris is aware that opinions differ when it comes to leaving old people in their own homes; the university chaplain and Bill's evangelical friends clearly differ in their assessment of his homosexuality and what he should do about it; and Shirley's friends are less impressed by her determination to carry on as before than many others in the church who can only admire her courage and wish there were more people like her. All these opinions, which could easily be multiplied, are held by Christians, and what we are left with is a simple example of the great variety of opinion which is everywhere to be found in the Christian community. Let us look at two more examples taken from the field of pastoral care.

One has to do with the third of our three questions, about how we can care for people helpfully and creatively, moving them on towards the provisional goals we have established. Part of the answer lies in the relationship between the caring and the cared for, a relationship not necessarily restricted to two people of course, though it will be convenient to discuss it as if it were. Some slight acquaintance with the history of pastoral care and contemporary thinking and writing about it soon reveals more than one opinion about what kind of relationship this should be. The following are caricatures rather than fair or carefully qualified accounts of any one person's view. There is first an authoritarian relationship. The 'pastor' knows on the good authority of the Church's teaching or the Bible the correct diagnosis of a person's ills, rather as a doctor knows his stuff in a case of physical illness, and knows the cure. Whether in the confessional or formal pastoral interview or a less formal visit to the home he will give his Christian counsel, confronting people with the gospel and fully expecting that it will be received with respect and complied with. The 'pastor' has authority and those he cares for will be obedient.[6] Second, there is the non-directive relationship in which the 'pastor', more often than not in a counselling situation, acts as a sounding board, listening carefully to what is said, carefully enough to reflect it back in comments and questions and sympathetically enough to reassure people that they are not unacceptable or condemned because of what they had to say. One thing the pastor does not do is offer advice. His aim rather is to give people an opportunity to regain a sense of their own worth and discover the resources that lie within themselves for dealing with their questions and problems.[7] A third type of relationship might be described as 'vulnerable' where the distinction between caring and cared for may become less clear. The 'pastor' is prepared to be recognized as someone who not only can be deeply affected by the feelings and troubles and aspirations of others so that he weeps and laughs with them, but who also shares their plight. He has similar strengths and weaknesses and is as much in need of their help as they are of his. He is not necessarily the strong man.[8] It would be misleading to suggest that these three approaches to the pastoral relationship cannot be reconciled in any way. Aspects of the first two, for example, can be combined to complement each other. The caring person can refuse to condemn without necessarily approving of everything that is said and can offer the stimulus of fresh resources as well as throw people back on their own. There remain, however, not just shades of opinion but real differences. The non-directive relationship declines to offer what the authoritarian relationship regards as its prime task to give, and neither of the first two puts the 'pastor' personally at risk as the third tends to do. He emerges as a strong, competent person well advised to keep his distance and not get too involved if he is to be of real help. R. S. Lee emphatically declares that the authoritarian minister cannot be a good counsellor.[9]

The other example of variety is historical. In their survey of pastoral care in the Christian tradition,[10] Charles Jaekle and William Clebsch acknowledge its vast range and attempt to reduce it to some kind of order by dividing Christian history into eight periods, suggesting that in each of them one of four main types of pastoral care comes to the fore without totally excluding the rest. They call these 'healing' or restoring the person to wholeness, 'sustaining' in situations such as bereavement and disability where troubles cannot be overcome and have to be endured, 'guiding' wayward behaviour and 'reconciling' or re-establishing good relationships between man and man and man and God. An account of the methods by which these 'pastoral' functions were carried out produces yet another long and varied list.

This variety or difference of opinion occurs wherever Christianity takes shape. It takes shape in pastoral care and it takes shape in the gospels we preach, in creeds and confessions, in liturgies and devotional exercises, in the organization of Christian communities or Churches, in ethical systems, in social and political responsibility and in the styles of life adopted by individual Christians. In every case we are not confronted with one gospel or creed or moral code or whatever, but with many. The variety can become somewhat bewildering as awareness grows of how the contemporary Church is made up of many traditions in so many lands and cultures, and of the Church's history over two thousand years. Even the New Testament is full of the same diversity with its several Gospels, its Johannine and Pauline and other ways of articulating the faith, and its different attitudes to such issues as the state and the law and to life in this world as against the next. All this variety makes it impossible to write a book about pastoral care and *the* Christian faith rather than pastoral care and Christian faith. There appears to be no such thing as *the* faith, only many Christian faiths.

The reasons for these diverse expressions of faith need not at this juncture detain us for long. Many of them are rooted in the conditions under which human beings have lived for as long as anyone can remember. We think differently and come to different conclusions because we do our thinking in response to the circumstances of our lives, and they change from one place to another and one generation to the next. Jaekle and Clebsch bring this out very well in relation to the changing emphases in pastoral care. 'Sustaining' came to the fore at an early stage when the Church believed the world was coming to an end and all its ills were to be endured briefly rather than overcome. 'Reconciling' dominated at a later stage when Church and Empire opposed each other and problems arose over those who renounced their faith under threat of persecution and the terms on which they should be forgiven and restored to Christian fellowship. 'Guidance' was of paramount importance in the Dark Ages when the Church confronted the uncivilized hordes of Northern Europe; and so on. Culture also contributes to variety. We inevitably draw on ideas that are to hand. The highly distinctive developments in pastoral care during this century owe almost everything to the cultural fascination with psychology and psychotherapy which followed hard on the heels of the Freudian revolution. Even within the same culture we put things differently because words and concepts that are familiar to our social group are not always familiar to everybody else's. We disagree because we can only tackle any issue with limited information and from a limited point of view. We cannot see or know everything. We also disagree because to a greater or lesser extent we bend the truth to suit ourselves. Culture, temperament, circumstances, human limitations and perversity all contribute to the multiplicity of our opinions, leaving the strong impression that we should be extremely wary of giving to any one of them the status of absolute truth or the last word on any subject. This adds weight to our decision not to give answers to the questions we have raised about pastoral care if doing so implies that there are correct answers to be had. With so many variable factors, most of them quite unavoidable, all answers must inevitably be relative, related to and influenced by the setting in which they were thrashed out, so that when the setting changes they change. Under the circumstances it is not easy to see what it would mean to tick off any answer as 'correct' and certainly not to think of it as Christian because it is correct.

Some will disagree. They may readily accept that when it comes to the details of Christian opinion-forming and decision-making there are too many non-religious factors and half-known quantities to be taken into account for us ever to cry dogmatically that one of many opinions is the correct one as far as Christians are concerned. At the circumference we must tolerate many points of view; but at the centre it is quite a different story. Here there are a number of abiding truths not relative opinions, and any expression of faith which claims to be Christian, be it gospel, creed, confession, liturgy, moral judgement or pastoral care, must conform to them. Examples of such central truths would be the doctrine of God as Trinity, of Christ as the incarnate Son of God, of man made in God's image, of creation and redemption and, in the moral sphere, the supreme value put on the kind of loving epitomized in the life of Jesus. Here are the essentials of Christian faith and if our opinions are in line with them they are Christian, otherwise they are not.

Without rejecting this line of argument entirely we must be aware of its difficulties. Whilst any Christian community is entitled to define what it means by the Christian faith at any one time and to include or exclude on that basis, it is not all that easy to list many truths that Christians have always used as defining characteristics of their faith; and what continuity there is may be more apparent than real because it is expressed in very general terms. We may have to agree that almost all Christians have believed in the Trinity and almost all in the incarnation, but their detailed explanations of what they mean by these things has varied a great deal, just as everyone approves of love but is ready to differ over what it actually means to love. And even here at the centre we are more ready to accept a measure of relativity than we used to be. Doctrines have to be remade because they were first made under cultural and historical conditions which have changed, so that what rang true once does not ring so true now. To judge anything as Christian by its conformity to abiding Christian truths may tend to rely too heavily on absolutes which don't exist. We are therefore inclined to reject one possible answer to the question: 'What is Christian pastoral care?' or indeed what makes anything Christian, namely that it conforms to a fixed notion of what is correct by Christian standards and is thereby orthodox.

Our discussion of the wide variety of opinion which is found wherever we look in the Christian Church strengthens the view that a more satisfactory understanding of orthodoxy, or orthopractice, and of what makes pastoral care Christian is to be found along lines we have already begun to explore. We have suggested that faith may transform and support, but that when it comes to reflecting on practice it should also inform. When it does, the outcome will be Christian pastoral care, not because we have arrived at acceptable conclusions but because in arriving at our conclusions whatever they may be we have taken faith deliberately into account.

A preliminary indication of what is involved in doing so might be given in terms of two central disciplines. The first is closely allied to what I take to be one of the earliest and simplest definitions of a Christian, and that is someone who takes Jesus as Lord, the supreme ruling principle of life. Everything is finally measured against that: not a set of doctrines but a person, dead and alive. Any expression of Christian faith, including any answers we give to our questions about pastoral care, will be the result of responding to many different things—hence the variety—but in addition they will all be a response to one thing or rather one Lord, and united in the attempt to be faithful to him.

The second discipline involved in taking faith into account is suggested by the variety and plurality of Christian opinion.

It reminds us forcibly that we are not Christians by ourselves but together with countless others in the past and present. They owe a similar allegiance to Jesus as Lord but they have understood him differently and they have made up many different faiths and forms of Christianity in the light of him. Any conclusions we make about pastoral care or any other aspect of Christian obedience worthy of the name must somehow take them seriously into account. This second discipline would, incidentally, take heed of the valid concerns of those who wish to test all Christian opinions against those essential teachings of the faith which appear to them to be unchanging. If it is true that over the centuries Christians have returned again and again to a number of central convictions, then if any member of the Christian community is going to take his fellow Christians seriously the persistence of those convictions cannot lightly be ignored; but that is not to say that those convictions are 'absolute truths' beyond question or reformulation.

It could be asked whether these two disciplines leave us far too tolerant of far too many opinions. One of the temptations of the relativist is to refuse to choose between various points of view because he is well aware that if he stood where others stand he would probably see things differently. He finds himself constantly allowing that something may be right or true for someone else even if it is not right or true 'for me'. Has our own sensitivity to the unavoidable reasons why Christians come to so many different conclusions put us in a similarly indecisive mood? Are we saying that as long as Christians refer to Christ and to other Christians in their reflection then there is little if anything to choose between them? Have we two criteria but no critical principle?

As we shall have to remind ourselves in a moment there are other reasons for choosing between one opinion and another, and deciding for example whether the relationship between the caring and the cared for should be authoritarian, non-directive or vulnerable, quite apart from any specifically Christian considerations; but unless they are to be no more than a formal nod in the right direction our two disciplines are perfectly capable of ruling certain opinions out of court or at the very least of putting serious question marks against them. Is it conceivable that 'anything goes' when we try to make sure that our pastoral care is 'Christlike and in it is no unChristlikeness at all'? And is it likely that if we expose ourselves to what our fellow Christians have to say to us we shall not soon realize that we have some serious rethinking to do in the light of their corrective and complementary remarks? To agree that rarely if ever shall we have grounds for totally dismissing an honestly arrived at point of view is very far from saying that rarely if ever shall we have good grounds for criticizing it.

Pastoral care then may become Christian pastoral care when exercised by Christians and by people sustained by Christian faith but also when the actual substance of it, what is actually done, is informed by a constant critical dialogue between the Christian and his Lord and the Christian and his community. The result will not necessarily be distinctive. Some write as if Christian practice, including the practice of pastoral care, becomes Christian only when it is different from everyone else's practice and pastoral care (compare John Cobb's comment about faith giving 'distinctive shape' to counselling) but it is Christian not because it always reaches distinctive conclusions but because it has distinctive points of reference.

In a later chapter we shall look at what it could mean to take Jesus our Lord seriously into account when we reflect on our practice, well aware of the difficulties involved in knowing much about him as he really was and making a loyal response to him. Before that we shall look at some of the ways in which what our fellow Christians have made of Jesus and of life in the light of Jesus is made available to us as resources and points of reference for our reflection. Two of them are relevant to all aspects of Christian obedience though we shall try to relate them particularly to pastoral care. They are Christian *doctrines* and what we shall call interpretative frameworks or *stories* about human experience. Two further resources are especially relevant to pastoral care. They are *theories* of pastoral care, sometimes called 'pastoral theologies', and *cases* or case studies of pastoral care. If we had been reflecting on other matters, on mission or ethics or the ministry, for example, we would have chosen other theories to talk about: theories of mission, moral or ethical theories, theories of ministry; and other case studies, more appropriate to our theme. We shall have to try to understand something about the nature of these resources for reflection before we can see to what extent and in what way they can be used.

Some may be alarmed to note that what might be regarded as the most important resource for Christian reflection has not been mentioned, and that is the Bible. The intention is not to leave it out of account but to see it for what it is. The Bible is not another additional resource quite different in kind from all the others we have mentioned. Rather it is a very early and especially interesting collection of resources. It bears witness to what Jesus was like, most notably in the Gospels. It contains a whole armoury of doctrines, in sections of Paul's letters such as Romans 1—8, and it tells 'stories' about what is going on in our human experience. One can be found in the opening passages of the letter to the Ephesians which talks about the growing unity of all things in Christ. The New Testament also develops a good many theories, of the Church for example and the state, and it is full of instances or cases of what Christians have actually thought and done on specific occasions, including cases of how they have exercised pastoral care. The Bible then can be referred to as we deal with each type of resource for reflection rather than as one on its own. Has it any special importance? A responsible answer to that question would involve us in a long discussion about biblical authority. Here we must be content to state that in our view it is not of any special importance because it is especially inspired in a way that other Christian resources, like a twentieth-century creed as against a Pauline creed, are not. And it is not of special importance because it is immune from the limiting factors we described earlier, which tend to make all Christian opinions including biblical opinions relative rather than absolute and provisional rather than final. Its special importance lies mainly in the fact that what we have in the New Testament are some of the very earliest responses to Jesus which survived the kind of critical dialogue within the Christian community of which we have been speaking. Some did not survive and were excluded from the canon of Scripture. Those which did are in most ways just like all the other responses that followed them in Christian history, except that they lie closer to Jesus himself, reflecting rather more of the freshness of his impact on his disciples and having a particular force and significance for us as a result.

Notes

1. In *Theology and Pastoral Care.* Fortress Press 1977.
2. ibid., p. 3.
3. ibid., p. 4.
4. *Three Issues in Ethics* (SCM Press 1970), pp. 89f.
5. See, for example, other books in this series and the series on Care and Counselling.
6. Something of this approach is reflected in Eduard Thurneysen, *A Theology of Pastoral Care.* John Knox Press 1963.
7. See, for example, Seward Hiltner, *Preface to Pastoral Theology.* Abingdon Press 1958.
8. Alastair Campbell, op.cit., and Frank Wright, *The Pastoral Nature of the Ministry* (SCM Press 1980), seem to favour this approach.
9. In *Principles of Pastoral Counselling* (SPCK 1980), pp. 126f.
10. *Pastoral Care in Historical Perspective.* Jason Aronson 1975.

FOUR

A Sense of Proportion

We have been arguing in favour of stronger links between pastoral care and Christian faith so that wherever possible faith not only transforms and supports those who care but actually informs what they do. Before going on to look more carefully at the Christian resources for informing our practice, such as the doctrines of the Church, we must pause however briefly and try to maintain a sense of proportion, lest having made too little of theology we now make too much. For the fact is that however many important things theology may have to say to us it is not all-knowing, and it is fairly easy to compile a long list of items of information which caring people will need to have but which no amount of referring to Jesus or the Christian creeds or any of the theological resources we mentioned is going to give them.

If we go back to our stories for a moment, if John is to be of much use he will need some facts and not just fears about Martin's job prospects inside the Church and out, and maybe a cool and realistic assessment of his abilities. David, or whoever eventually helps Peter and Kate to sort out their relationship, will need some insight into what is going on between them and what makes each of them tick, and if they decide to part they will need a well-informed lawyer not a well-informed Christian. Shirley probably needs some reassurance from a doctor and advice from a friendly bank manager, and anyone who cares for her will need to get the measure of her determination—not just the strength of it but why she drives herself quite as hard as she does. The Church has a good deal to say about Bill's homosexuality but it cannot tell him all he needs to know, or how countless others are learning to live with it in a more tolerant but often unsympathetic and sneering atmosphere. Gordon will need a lesson in social history and social dynamics if he is to understand Joseph's and Daniel's sense of alienation, and another in politics and community development if he is to improve their lot. And faith will not be able to explain fully to Doris why old age is feared and dishonoured in this society though not in all, nor will it provide the skills of the adult educationalist to foster the potential which she discovers in Phyllis and herself. It seems then, to put it formally, that the disciplines of psychology, law, medicine, education, economics, politics, behavioural studies and history, to say nothing of careful observation, technical know-how and experience must supply information which Christianity as such does not have to share.

To put it another way, the theologian, anxious that his discipline should have its proper place, must not be heard denying the extent to which he relies upon and needs to work with others, adopting what is often referred to as the inter-disciplinary approach; or the immense value of contributions to pastoral care in which theological voices are scarcely raised at all. To take but one example, in *You Alone Care*[1] Heather McKenzie is concerned in a very down to earth way for the elderly relative referred to as the 'dependant', and the caring person whom she pictures as a single woman looking after her mother. Her limited aims are to make the mother's last years happy and serene and to alleviate the considerable burdens which the daughter has to carry. In other words she wants to make life easier for both. Her book is not full of theology but of valuable information falling roughly into two categories which correspond in turn to two of the three basic questions which arise when we reflect on practice: 'What are we dealing with?' and 'How best can we help?'

In relation to the first, the book helps the daughter to identify the kind of situation she finds herself in with all its implications when she has to decide whether to stay at home and look after her mother or admit her to residential care, whether to carry on working or leave her job, whether to take mother to live with her or go and live with mother. It alerts the daughter to the moral pressures which will be put on her from time to time by other members of the family as well as the dependant, to the resentment she is likely to feel, to the signs of her own weariness and failing health and the stages of her grieving when mother eventually dies. The book also helps the daughter to understand her mother's situation as she gradually loses her independence, her health, the dignity that goes with privacy, and becomes prone to bouts of depression as her activities and her circle of friends are increasingly restricted. Heather McKenzie contributes to pastoral care by helping the caring person to see these things clearly for what they are, just as David in one of our stories felt he needed to do when talking to Peter and Kate about the growing tensions in their marriage.

The second type of material in the book suggests to the single woman how she could respond creatively to her own and her mother's needs. If she is to care for her mother then she must preserve some sort of life for herself and have adequate rest and regular breaks. These points are made repeatedly. Advice about caring for her mother ranges from hints about how to ease the worst anxieties of an old person still living on her own, to elementary instructions in home nursing, to the best ways of handling the emotional crises that are bound to arise. 'Knowing what to do', Heather McKenzie remarks almost naively, 'can be of immeasurable help'.[2] No doubt Gordon in another of our stories would have agreed as he wondered how to rescue Daniel from the fate of the young unemployed!

Not one single piece of advice given in Heather McKenzie's book owes anything to Christian faith in the sense that faith informed her about the truth of these situations or told her what to do. All of them could have been and doubtless were derived from professional training, considerable experience and common sense. Faith appears to have little to say. It is mentioned only three times in the book and where it is it is understood as playing a supportive role: 'Faith can be a great sustainer, and many carers get through a heavy caring burden by having a deep faith.'[3]

I for one have no complaints about the apparently minor role which faith has to play in this particular account of pastoral care, supporting rather than informing in a case where information of a different kind is of far greater use. On many occasions faith must realize that it does not know what to say and give way to those better qualified to analyse what is going on and suggest what is most likely to achieve the desired results.

We spoke earlier of what we would regard as a 'Christian' opinion or decision about pastoral care. It is one that takes the resources of the Christian community into account. Keeping a sense of proportion we might also venture to speak of a 'good' decision about pastoral care as one which has wisely taken other relevant resources into account and has not been made in unnecessary ignorance. The two are not the same. A 'Christian' opinion need not be a 'good' one and a 'good' one need not, as in Heather McKenzie's case, be 'Christian' any more than it need be incompatible with Christianity. Our aim must be to make decisions which are both 'Christian' and 'good'!

Notes

1. SPCK 1980; others include R. S. Lee, *Principles of Pastoral Counselling* (SPCK 1980), which could be seen as a typical example of the psychologist ruling the roost; Kenneth Leech, *Pastoral Care and the Drug Scene* (SPCK 1970), which contains comparatively little material of an explicitly theological kind; and Michael Jacobs, *Still Small Voice* (SPCK 1982), explaining techniques which apply to pastoral settings but virtually excluding any reference to theology.
2. McKenzie, op. cit., p. 117.
3. ibid., p. 136.

FIVE

The Relevance of Doctrine

The doctrines of the Church are one of the forms in which what our fellow Christians have made of Christ is made available to us. The major ones have things to say about God, creation, evil and the fall, man, the person and work of Christ (who he was and what he did), salvation, the Holy Spirit, the Church, the Kingdom and the last things such as death, judgement, heaven and hell. Our argument is that if pastoral care is to be 'Christian' convictions such as these must be taken into account. They must inform our reflection on practice.

One of the most difficult tasks, in view of the divorce between theology and practice, may be to convince ministers and lay people of what may seem obvious to professional theologians, that Christian doctrine is relevant to their practical concerns. Do they have anything to say, they might ask, about the situations which confront us, the aims and objectives we might adopt and about how we might most effectively achieve them? Do they speak to the basic questions which arise, as people like Heather McKenzie in her practical book and doctors and psychiatrists with their diagnosis and treatments so clearly do?

In a number of cases they may not take too much persuading that the answer is 'Yes'. The Christian doctrine of man talks about the kind of people we are dealing with. It asserts among other things that they are not self-made or self-explanatory or self-sufficient but limited, creaturely beings tied in many ways to nature and each other. They are not however wholly determined. They can rise above many of the restrictions imposed on them and choose to live in the loving relationships with one another and with God for which they were made. The fact that invariably they do not, but choose instead to go against their outgoing natures, become self-centred and depend overmuch on themselves, is the major source of their unhappiness and the reason why they are so often destructive and not creative. Remarks like these add to, and on occasions contradict, the information we have from other sources about an ageing relative and her bouts of depression, or Shirley's anxieties, Bill's homosexuality or Daniel's understandable resentment.

Similarly it is not too difficult to believe that if we explored the Christian doctrine of salvation with its ideas about freedom and wholeness and reconciliation, or the doctrine of the Kingdom with its visions of what it is like to live under the rule of God in harmony with his will, we should uncover plenty of hints about the proper aims and objectives of Christian pastoral care.

But many doctrines appear to be less than promising material for reflection. Some, like the doctrines of creation and the fall and the last things, appear to talk about events which lie in the past or the future but not about our current affairs. They talk about what has happened and what will happen but not what is happening now. Others deal with God and Christ and the Holy Spirit, not with people like us or Peter or Daniel or Phyllis. They talk about anyone but the people we want to talk about. The doctrines of incarnation and atonement refer to activities which can never be ours. It is God who was incarnate in Jesus not us, and he alone atones for our sin through the death of his Son. Often doctrine sounds as if it is wrapped up in a world of its own and a history of its own where a Trinitarian God sorts out his own internal relationships and wins man's salvation by doing a deal with himself and honouring his own sense of justice without involving man at all. Much of this talk seems very remote from our efforts to care for one another. Can the situation be redeemed?

Attempts have been made from time to time to write off all theology or talk about God as in effect anthropology: thinly veiled or heavily disguised talk about man. It is little more than an expression of our wishful thinking or a dressed-up way of stating what we value most. Such attempts will be judged unsuccessful by those who believe in a godly reality other than ourselves and not just of our making, and that theology is part of our response to it. As such, we are not always at the centre of its interests and it is not always directly relevant to our immediate concerns. It has about it quite properly a note of irrelevance, but it is not so totally irrelevant or unrelated as it might often appear.

To begin with, the preoccupation of some doctrines with the past is more apparent than real. The doctrines of creation and the fall, as presented in the early chapters of the Bible, sound like accounts of what happened when the world began. But it is only their way of talking. They are really the story of everyman with the joy and responsibility of being the crown of a good creation, and his awareness that things are not as they should be in the world, of paradise lost or never really found. Old as these stories are and without denying that many have regarded them as histories of the earliest days of life on earth, they were from the start attempts to explain the world which the story teller was living in: so good and yet so evil. They are commentaries on the present written in the past tense, just as aspects of the doctrine of the last things comment in the future tense on the significance of the present, where a great deal, eternity in fact, may hang on our decisions.

Even where a doctrine does not speak directly about our world in whatever tense, there will be corollaries of it which do. The doctrine of the Trinity has nothing to say about the people we are trying to care for or how we should care for them. It is doubtful that it can even be pressed into service as a vote for good relationships or as exemplifying the solidarity (three in one) and respect for individual identity (one in three) which should characterize them. It is talking about the inner nature of God. But one of its many corollaries is that God as spirit is immanent in our human affairs, and we have already suggested that it could say quite a lot to us about the growing estrangement between, for example, two people whose marriage is falling apart. It suggests that there is another factor to be reckoned with in any such situation, resources striving for unity beyond those which are readily apparent, so that where we seem to have exhausted all our ability to communicate, understand and reconcile there may yet be other possibilities; or that if we press ours into service something may be achieved over and above what we have it in us to achieve. Again, the doctrine of God speaks mainly about God not as he is in himself but as he is related to us; and whether he is a relation who regards us as members of the family or as outsiders who must win their seats at the table, and whether we are answerable to him or to others or to no one but ourselves could make all the difference to our self-understanding.

Doctrines which appear to be talking about what was true only once, like the incarnation or resurrection, can also be understood as talking about what is always true, without denying what was once true in a special or particular way. One account of the person of Christ or who he was, as old as the Gospel of John, actively encourages us to think like this. John calls Jesus the Word made flesh (1.14) by which he might well mean that what we discern in this one man's living and dying is the truth (14.6) about all living and dying. If the world makes sense then here is the clue that makes sense of it. Here the true word is spoken about man and about God and about the relationship between them. Here we see what humanity is like at its best, what God is always like and how he deals with man and expects man to respond to God. On this basis some of the great doctrinal words which have been used to characterize the ministry of Jesus become insights into the ongoing character of all human life. If God is incarnate in Jesus he can be thought of as incarnate in us all, for one of the abiding truths about God is that he comes to dwell among us, as the doctrine of the Spirit confirms. If God takes in Jesus the form of a servant then it may be argued that it is always such a God with whom we have to deal, or that the odds are ultimately for us and not against us. If Jesus is raised from the dead then it can be said that God is at work to raise men to life all the time. So we believe not mainly in *the* incarnation and *the* resurrection but in incarnation and resurrection as characteristic of all human occasions including the ones we are confronted with in pastoral care.[1] Such an understanding of the Word as being true of our lives as well as of the life of Jesus is not meant to obscure the fact that his life was also very different from ours. To explain how would be to embark on a full-scale discussion of the doctrine of the person of Christ, but one simple way of understanding the difference without denying the continuity is to think of Jesus as the exemplification of what it means to be a man living in relation to God. He epitomizes our two-natured existence, human and divine, at its best, as no one else to our knowledge has so far done.

The most fundamental point to be made about the relevance of doctrine puts it firmly in the business of informing our pastoral care. It could be argued that doctrine is always made out of our experience in this world, including our experience of Christ, and is therefore full of information about it, since there is nothing else to make it from. But to put it less controversially, even when its immediate subject matter is far removed from our ordinary everyday experience, doctrine still has to draw on it in order to understand and then find ways of expressing what it wants to say.

The best illustration of this I know is in F. W. Dillistone's *The Christian Understanding of Atonement,*[2] a book which, for our purposes, has the particular merit of dealing with a doctrine which appears to be irrelevant on two counts. First, it is teaching us about something which happened in the past when Jesus died on the cross. Second, it is teaching us about something which God did for us and not which we can do for anyone else. Some Christians would be adamant that these points are in no sense disadvantageous but of the essence of the atonement. It was and can be none of our doing, or else salvation begins to be a matter of works and not of grace; and it is a once-for-all event never to be repeated because it has done everything that needs to be done. But even if we grant all this absolutely it still remains true that the doctrine of the atonement is busy talking about our experience and the experience of those we care for even as it attempts to explain the work of Christ.

Dillistone describes the way in which a doctrine of atonement (for there are several) arises as an interplay between fact and a 'theory' or 'framework of interpretation' or 'range of comparison'. If we are faced with a fact like the death of Jesus on the cross, however exceptional or unusual to us it may be, we should not be able to speak about it at all if it were literally true that we had never seen anything like it before. It would be totally incomprehensible. We can talk about it only because, although we have never seen anything quite like it before, it does bear comparison with what is already familiar. And so we make comparisons as we try to explain, or, as Dillistone puts it, we 'see the fact within a certain range of comparison'. We say that this unusual event reminds us of certain patterns of experience, in this case where suffering and death have somehow provided the pathway to the enhancement and enrichment of life, which have recurred again and again in human history and happen to be known to us (there are others of which we know nothing) as we set about the business of explaining. Among earlier Christians, for example, the crucifixion was thought to be rather like an act of redemption whereby at considerable cost freedom was won from slavery, or an act of justification whereby honour having been done the accused could stand acquitted, or an act of sacrifice whereby one life having been offered up another could be given back or spared. The unfamiliar is explained in terms of the familiar though, as Dillistone points out, that does not leave the familiar untouched. Views about sacrifice may be changed by the new fact which has arrived on the scene, just as the fact is seen to be not quite so new once compared to the tradition of sacrifice.

This account of Dillistone's argument may still leave us feeling that the doctrine of atonement is remote from our involvement with people like Martin and Bill and Joseph and Phyllis. This is partly because we have illustrated his general point by referring to the ranges of comparison used by earlier Christians as they created some of the classic theories of atonement. They no longer work for us quite so well as they did for them, though if we explored them carefully they contain ideas about how people are set free and made whole which still ring true.

In *The Minister and the Care of Souls*[3] Daniel Day Williams works in exactly the way that Dillistone has described but draws on a more contemporary 'range of comparison' or 'framework of interpretation' and one which comes directly out of the field of pastoral care. In Jesus, he explains, we experience the grace of God at work finding a way out for us from the bondage of sin. We have vitiated our own natures as people made for God and each other. We have become self-sufficient and self-concerned and we are to some extent responsible even though the measure of any one person's responsibility is difficult to judge. But we are unable to extricate ourselves from bondage. It is Christ who sets us free and makes us at-one with God, ourselves and our neighbours. But how does grace work? How are we set free? Traditional doctrines of atonement try to explain how we are given this opportunity to live in a new way but Williams is critical of them because they are often so impersonal. The classic theory about a victory over evil likens the atonement to a battle in which we are not involved. Others speak of legal penalties almost as if once sufficient punishment has been meted out the conditions for our release have been met. Such ideas need supplementing if not wholly replacing by more personal images.

At this point Williams turns to the world not of military conquests or legal requirements or sacrificial ritual, as the early Christians did, but to that of psychotherapy and the concept of 'acceptance'. The gift we receive through the work of Christ which releases us from sin is something like the gift offered by the counsellor who allows the troubled person no longer in possession of himself to relive what he has been and look for a new understanding of himself in an atmosphere which does not threaten rejection. Of crucial importance, says Williams, is the ability of the counsellor to take the feelings of the other person sympathetically into his own being as 'a deliberate and constructive act of self-identification'. In some such way Christ identifies with us and releases us. Again Williams agrees with Dillistone that the two are not exactly alike and just as the familiar experience may help us to understand the unfamiliar so the unfamiliar, the new fact, may make us think again about the familiar. Psychological acceptance, for example, is criticized by some but not all for failing to take seriously enough the idea of judgement and the need to acknowledge personal guilt. It may be too accepting and so fall short of the total giving and total demand, total identification and total transcendence, of the one who is 'lifted up' for our sakes. But it remains true that the atoning work of Christ 'has its reflections in our human experience at the point where men offer loyal understanding and care to one another in the midst of human evil'.[4]

If doctrines of atonement and other doctrines do take into

themselves such insights drawn from a more familiar world, they can be expected to yield those insights up again if we patiently investigate the framework of interpretation which they have exploited. In this instance teaching about what many would firmly hold to be a once-for-all event in the past can be expected to teach us or certainly remind us of the kind of activities including identification, acceptance and self-sacrifice which experience suggests are most likely to help and to heal when we reflect on how best to care for people in the present. In other words the doctrine addresses our question about what we can do to move on a situation effectively and creatively towards the goals we have in mind. These insights are not, as we have said, yielded up again just as they were. We do not go round in circles incorporating familiar understandings into doctrines only to disentangle them again when we might have made use of them directly and saved time. In the encounter, in this case between our human experience and the fact of Christ's great work, his work is better understood but our understanding of our experience is also changed.

We have been trying to show how Christian doctrine is more relevant to our reflection on pastoral care and our Christian obedience in general than might at first appear. But if it is often talking about the same questions, is it talking about them in the same way? How do these doctrinal observations relate to all the other information we require if we are to make 'good' decisions, and to the remarks of the psychiatrist or doctor or social worker or some other experienced practitioner who in effect says 'This is what is wrong' or 'This is the truth of the matter' and 'This is the best way to deal with it'? Is there any possibility of a conversation?

A crude distinction might be made to begin with between statements of fact and statements which go beyond the facts. Statements of fact describe what is there to be seen by everyone if they had an equal chance to see it. It may be a current state of affairs or what happened on some occasion in the past or how something works in a mechanistic chain of cause and effect. An account of them might be called 'historical' or 'scientific'. They are strictly speaking non-controversial, and based on evidence which can be made available. Statements which go beyond the facts talk about their importance, the values to be placed on them, about the real significance and purpose of what has happened. They try to interpret and make sense of things by knocking them into coherent and understandable shapes. Precisely because what they say adds to what can be observed and does not simply repeat it, such statements are more controversial. We are not bound to accept them. Some would prefer not to call them statements at all but opinions or beliefs.

To give two examples: the report that Jesus died during the governorship of Pontius Pilate is historical fact. The doctrine of atonement which we have been discussing tries to explain the significance of his dying and is an interpretation of the fact. The variety of doctrines of atonement in the Christian Church and the quite different interpretations of the death of Christ outside the Church show how controversial such an interpretation can be. The same set of facts can be interpreted in more than one way. Again, the report that the Titanic sank on her maiden voyage is historical fact, and if we could recover the evidence we could also give a factual account of why it happened. The suggestion that God has to allow this sort of thing to happen if there is to be any sort of freedom for man is part of an attempt to explain why it happened or was allowed to happen at a quite different level, and one with which many people would strongly disagree. It is an interpretation which goes well beyond the evidence.

Now it is tempting to say that the sort of information we cannot afford to ignore if we are to make 'good' decisions about pastoral care is of the first, factual kind, whereas the doctrines which must be allowed to inform our reflection if the outcome is to be 'Christian' are of the second. They go beyond the facts and are in the business of telling us what they mean. After all, Heather McKenzie's book, which we decided was full of the first kind of material, does appear to deal on the whole with careful, even clinical descriptions of people's physical and emotional conditions, and with technical advice about basic nursing procedures. It is factual like the job prospects for Martin and Daniel in our stories and the medical report that will be of interest to anyone with a sensible concern for Shirley, or the truth about homosexuality and whether homosexuals are born or made which the chaplain will be well advised to be familiar with if she is to have a useful conversation with Bill.

But such a division between Christian teaching and what others have to say to us would be over simple and misleading, and for three reasons. First, it would suggest that Christian doctrines have nothing to do with facts at all whereas they do. They may go beyond them but they do claim to be interpreting them, and whilst the facts may bear more than one interpretation they won't bear just any interpretation. Doctrines will never entirely fit the evidence but they cannot play fast and loose with it by making quite arbitrary comments. Secondly, purely factual statements are few and far between as we soon realize when technical experts disagree. The evidence does not put the matter beyond doubt. Value judgements often lie not far beneath the surface.[5] Historians, psychologists, sociologists, doctors, politicians and many others we recognized as useful informants, all deal in theories and frameworks which interpret the data they collect. Even the most severely factual, sometimes called 'scientific' accounts rest on massive assumptions about the reliability of our observations and the intelligibility of the universe. Third, it is not only that facts give rise to theories, but our theories, or the assumptions we unconsciously make about the world and the interpretative frameworks we put upon it, affect the way we see the facts. That point might well strike home to Gordon as he gets increasingly concerned about Daniel the black unemployed teenager who has begun to turn criminal behaviour into a way of life. The 'fact' is that if people go on breaking the law as Daniel has done we shall all suffer. But the 'facts' are different when seen through Daniel's eyes. Once the law is broken he and others like him might begin to suffer a little less, for on his frame of reference the law is not an impartial referee which operates in the best interests of everyone. Starting from different assumptions we see things differently and carry away different reports which we all claim to be factual accounts of what happened!

Instead of dividing statements into those which deal with facts and those which go beyond the facts, and putting Christian doctrine among the latter and what most of our other informants have to say among the former, it is more accurate to think of them all as speaking much the same language, containing similar elements ranging from facts or as near to them as we can get, through theories which organize them into orderly accounts of what has been observed, through explanations of what has happened at say the level of cause and effect, to the kind of interpretative frameworks and value judgements which might provide explanations of a very different kind. The emphasis may come at a different point but the range is much the same. Christian doctrine may appear to lie towards one end of it whilst what the local doctor tells Shirley about her health or John finds out about Martin's job prospects is at the other, but they are not so totally different in kind as not to be on speaking terms.

Alive to this possibility, we may be able to see more clearly the points at which Christian doctrine must grant other disciplines their autonomy or right to speak and take note of what they have to say, recognizing that it has no real grounds on which to quarrel, and the points at which comparisons and contradictions are in order. Facts can be pitted against facts and faith can quarrel with faith, but a faith confronted with facts it has not considered before is vulnerable and must pause for thought. Broadly speaking, faith will try to come to terms with facts because what it believes in general it must be able to believe about them, but it will keep an eye open for the explanations and assumptions which appear to go beyond the facts and measure up to them with explanations and assumptions of its own. Where there are none or very few it will be able to add a new dimension to what has already been said.

For example, two familiar answers to the question 'What are we dealing with?' are 'sickness' and 'sin'. The first might be supplied by a doctor or a psychiatrist, the second is the voice of Christian doctrine, though both are often expressed as commonsense opinions. It is quite likely that there is no great disagreement between them. Both affirm that all is not well, though we should note that even here we are dealing with something more than a straightforward observation; and their accounts of what has gone wrong may simply be complementary: elements of sickness and sinfulness are bound up together, exacerbating one another.

But they could represent two very different assessments of

a situation leading to appropriate or quite inappropriate responses as the case may be. If it is interpreted entirely in terms of 'sickness'[6] then those involved cannot be held responsible; if we are dealing with 'sin' and wilful perversity then they can. Curiously enough, when it comes to asking how far those involved can contribute to putting matters right, opinion is often divided on both sides. The sick have to be healed by outside agencies, and yet they can contribute to their own healing. The sinner must repent and yet suffers from the bondage of the will and must be saved by grace. Both the sense of being helpless and of being able to help ourselves strike chords in our experience.

The area of disagreement could be quite acute if it is claimed that all unacceptable behaviour is rooted in unfortunate experiences in childhood and infancy so that any hint of blame will only lead to further repression and make matters worse. There are factual elements here which everyone who wishes to set about castigating people for their sins must examine with care and, if substantiated, treat with respect. Going well beyond the facts to profounder explanations we may come to the conclusion not so much that those who talk of 'sickness' disagree with those who talk of 'sin' but that the battle cannot be joined because at this level the former have little to say. They may be able to account for our sickness at the comparatively trivial level of cause and effect but not for the very existence of those faults and misfortunes in our experience which are so fundamental that mothers and babies, parents and children, regularly fail to establish relationships which make for mature rather than infantile personalities in later life. Why does it all keep going so terribly wrong? If doctrine breaks the silence by saying it is due to man disobeying God it has to admit to a certain amount of embarrassment about locating the moment when that disobedience first occurs. What we have here are not two faiths arguing with each other, since only one appears to have entered the field with its strong belief in human culpability. We have one faith, Christian faith, with certain aspects of experience on its side, and others it finds less easy to live with but whose reality is hard to deny. Pastoral wisdom may in the end decide to build on the common ground acknowledging the intransigent nature of many of our ills and sorrows, never resolved by apportioning blame and instructing people to change their ways, and taking seriously both the depth of our need for outside resources generously given and the strong probability that we can nevertheless share in our own healing and restitution as those who are more than the victims of circumstance.

Turning to a second, related example, we have already referred to the therapeutic principle of 'acceptance' which allows negative feelings to be acknowledged and expressed within a non-judgemental and understanding relationship and noted how similar it is to some of the notes sounded by the Christian doctrine of atonement, so much so that a writer like Daniel Day Williams can use it as a 'range of comparison'. There may even be profounder similarities in that the therapist like the gospel can sometimes be heard to acknowledge that what is involved is not only accepting a person but also the suffering they can inflict on those who make themselves vulnerable. We shall not stop to discuss possible areas of disagreement over, for example, the accepting person's lack of discrimination. They may in any case be more apparent than real. 'Acceptance' does not mean 'approval' but the refusal to reject and condemn even when we disapprove. And it is doubtful that any careful process of bringing to expression so-called negative feelings can be devoid of the element of judgement, of seeing things for what they are, of sifting wheat from chaff, on which the gospel insists.

The psychotherapist's decision to 'accept' and the Christian decision to 'forgive' which sound so much alike illustrate well the levels at which two such different informants can converse and decide in the end whether to agree. The psychotherapist makes a clear appeal to facts, though the facts may seem rather less objective to many when dealing with such a subjective world. His experience has led him to the conclusion that acceptance allows the positive and recuperative psychic powers to emerge and do their work. The point is put quite plainly by Carl Rogers:

> Let me explain what I mean when I say that I am going to summarise what we 'know'. I mean that I will limit my statements to those for which we have objective empirical evidence.
>
> When the therapist is experiencing a warm, positive and

acceptant attitude toward what *is* in the client, this facilitates change. It involves the therapist's genuine willingness for the client to be whatever feeling is going on in him at that moment — fear, confusion, pain, pride, anger, hatred, love, courage, or awe. It means that the therapist cares for the client, in a non-possessive way.

It means that he prizes the client in a total rather than a conditional way. By this I mean that he does not simply accept the client when he is behaving in certain ways, and disapprove of him when he behaves in other ways. It means an outgoing positive feeling without reservations, without evaluations. The term we have come to use for this is unconditional positive regard. Again research studies show that the more this attitude is experienced by the therapist, the more likelihood there is that therapy will be successful.[7]

Here are facts in the form of a piece of technical advice about what works, and those who challenge them at that level as some Christians might wish to do, and as some therapists have done by introducing a measure of confrontation into their counselling, will also need to support their claims with 'objective empirical evidence'.

Leaving aside the interesting possibility that Carl Rogers' overall approach goes beyond those factual considerations (we shall return to it in a later chapter) and that there could therefore be a faith to faith encounter, Christianity will have to come to terms with the evidence presented to it by the therapist. Should it wish to affirm, as it has not infrequently done, that redemption involves on occasions the condemnation and ruthless exclusion of the sinner as well as the sin, it must be ready to do so in spite of the evidence that such procedures consistently make matters worse. What it believes, it must be prepared to believe about the world in front of it.

But although the Christian must take seriously the reasons why the therapist decides to accept, his own decision to forgive is more than a piece of technical wisdom upheld or rejected according to the results of further experiment. Forgiveness is to be practised where it manifestly does not work: '"Lord, how often shall my brother sin against me, and I forgive him? As many as seven times?" Jesus said to him, "I do not say to you seven times, but seventy times seven"'

(Matt. 18.21f). It is advocated on other grounds than observable results. Perhaps forgiveness and the kind of relationships that go with it are valued whatever the results. Perhaps there is a confidence, ill-founded in unbelieving eyes, that however much it is despised in the here and now it will win through in the end and does correspond with the way the world works, but whatever it is that inspires the Christian it goes beyond what he can demonstrate, and if he is to talk further with the psychotherapist it will be to ask what in turn inspires him to make his own persistent and at times heroic efforts to help his client.

We have been trying to illustrate that there are similar elements in what all our informants have to say to us and that, if we remember the proper relation of faith to facts (it must take account of them but is not wholly determined by them) and allow like to talk with like, there can be a fruitful conversation in which they may reinforce, complement or contradict each other. Insofar as all statements go beyond the facts to some extent it might be fair to say that theology differs by setting out to go beyond them as far as it possibly can, rooting its responses to questions about pastoral care in the deepest and broadest considerations. Others cannot keep out of this territory but their business is not to venture into it quite so far. The psychologist has little to say by way of explaining the persistent flaw in human personality whereby deprivation breeds deprivation; the therapist does not tell us why it matters that we should grow up to maturity. Heather McKenzie's aims are strictly limited: to alleviate the burdens of single persons and make the last years of their elderly relatives happy and serene; an experienced social worker suggests that one of the differences between the caseworker and the priest or pastor is that the caseworker solves specific problems and leaves it at that whilst the priest has a bigger aim seeing 'the significance of the crises and the problem solving', and helping 'to set the sorrows, joys, sins, and struggles of our life in an eternal framework'.[8]

Christian doctrine, then, does not deal with faith and nothing else, and it is not the only dealer in faith, but its faith may be more comprehensive. It tries to set the contributions of science and technology and education and the like, along with experience and common sense, in the widest possible framework where parts can be seen in relation to the whole and matters of relative importance are not absolutized to threaten those which concern us above all; where the search for salvation may have to override the search for long life, health and peace of mind, and where the limits of enquiry are nothing short of the purpose and will of the indescribable God.

Where faith does meet faith and doctrines are involved in a genuine clash of opinion, how much notice should we take of them? As Christians we shall take a great deal. Doctrines are not the private beliefs of individuals or the opinions however weighty of theologians. They are the convictions of a community. As such they have the support of many people and they have been tried and tested and not found entirely wanting in a great many situations over a long period of time. For that reason alone we shall not lightly set them aside. In addition they are inspired (to what extent we have still to discuss) by the living and dying of one whom we respect above all others, so that there is behind them a measure of his personal authority; and during the long course of their development from the earliest Christian communities of New Testament times down to the present day we believe they have benefited from the guidance of the Holy Spirit leading the Church into all the truth.

But if we respect Christian doctrines we shall not respect them too much. We have already seen how any expression of Christianity, including doctrine, is bound to be limited and relative to the historical, cultural and personal circumstances in which it arose and took shape. If they change, as they frequently do, then it will have to be reshaped and remade. There is no great gulf fixed here between the knowledge we have derived though our faith in Christ and the knowledge gained through our secular observations and experience. It is also impossible to give absolute guarantees about the truth of a doctrine. Any authority to which we appeal such as the Bible or the Church is as conditioned as the doctrine itself, and if we believe that the Holy Spirit guarantees its reliability we must recognize that we are giving authority to one doctrine only by referring to another and simply relocating our problem rather than solving it. Finally we shall not treat any doctrine with absolute respect because, as we have seen, like anything else we claim to know about our world, it is vulnerable to the facts of which it tries to make sense. We have a good deal of confidence that it is talking sense because it has been engaging with these facts of life for a very long time, but we also know that it has had to be reformulated more than once when it was no longer taking account of them sufficiently well. Any moment of reflection on obedience may be the occasion when that happens again.

Notes

1. J. A. T. Robinson, *The Human Face of God* (SCM Press 1973), especially chapter 7; and H. A. Williams, *True Resurrection.* Mitchell Beazley 1972.
2. Nisbet 1968.
3. Harper and Row 1977, chapter 4.
4. ibid., p. 91.
5. The point was brought home forcibly in relation to counselling and social casework by Paul Halmos, *The Faith of the Counsellors* (Constable 1965), and is readily accepted by for example Jean Heywood, *Casework and Pastoral Care* (SPCK 1967), p. 40, and Michael Jacobs, op. cit., pp. 128f.
6. cf. R. S. Lee, op.cit., chapter 8.
7. *On Becoming a Person* (Constable 1977), pp. 60 and 62.
8. Jean Heywood, op. cit., p. 69.

SIX

The Stories of Our Lives

———

We have been arguing that faith expressed in the form of doctrine is relevant to our reflection on pastoral care. It is often talking about the issues we raise, and it does so in a way which is not altogether different from that of others who offer us, not specifically Christian, but equally important insights and information. Apart from a few illustrative asides, however, we have said very little about what these doctrines have to teach us. If we did set it out we should have a welter of material for not only are there a fair number of doctrines, but each one must be regarded as a heading below which is a wealth of detail and variety of opinion. Here is an example of the complexity we must not deny but which makes for difficulties, since if pastoral care as we have characterized it is the business of all Christian people, if all are pastors, they must all be 'theologians' as well. Their practice must be informed by their faith and take Christian doctrine into account; but how are they going to handle it once it has been received and assimilated, if only to carry it about?

The difficulty about receiving it must be left on one side for the time being until we come to look at doing theology in community and the special contribution of ministers and clergy. The second difficulty can be eased by turning to another set of resources for reflection. I have called them stories or interpretative frameworks. They differ from doctrines in a number of ways. They are not a series of rather flat statements or propositions as doctrines tend to be. They are more like narratives often built around a single image. As such they are easier to remember since the story can be elaborated from the image. They may also be more influential, appealing not only to the intellect but to the imagination, to the heart as well as to the head. Another difference is that whereas a doctrine comments on one area of our experience of life in God's world a story is far more comprehensive and might even attempt a rounded commentary on them all. A single, memorable image or a really good story may then become the carrier for us of the whole substance of Christian doctrinal teaching, offering everyday theologians a practical way of setting their questions about pastoral care and Christian obedience in the widest possible framework.[1]

An example of such a story can be found in some familiar and oft-quoted lines from T. S. Eliot's *Four Quartets.*

The wounded surgeon plies the steel
That questions the distempered part;
Beneath the bleeding hands we feel
The sharp compassion of the healer's art
Resolving the enigma of the fever chart.

Our only health is the disease
If we obey the dying nurse
Whose constant care is not to please
But to remind of our, and Adam's curse,
And that, to be restored, our sickness must grow worse.

The whole earth is our hospital
Endowed by the ruined millionaire,
Wherein, if we do well, we shall
Die of the absolute paternal care
That will not leave us, but prevents us everywhere.

The chill ascends from feet to knees,
The fever sings in mental wires.
If to be warmed, then I must freeze
And quake in frigid purgatorial fires
Of which the flame is roses, and the smoke is briars.

The dripping blood our only drink,
The bloody flesh our only food:
In spite of which, we like to think
That we are sound, substantial flesh and blood —
Again, in spite of that, we call this Friday good.

I do not comment on what the poem meant to Eliot, only on what it means to me. The story of our lives and the image which embraces everything ('The whole earth is our hospital') is one of *healing.* The reality of the human situation is that we are far from well. 'Adam's curse' is a 'sickness', a distemper, a fever. As the poet affirms elsewhere, 'all shall be well and all manner of things shall be well', but things 'must grow worse' before they can get better. In some mysterious way health lies in the disease or at least in a painful form of treatment, 'sharp', 'purgatorial', 'bloody', chilling and fiery. The surgeon or nurse who heals us, as omnipresent as the disease ('the absolute paternal care that will not leave us, but prevents us everywhere') appears to suffer from it just as we do. 'Wounded' and 'dying' his own 'bloody flesh' does not escape unscathed when exercising the healer's art.

A second story is told by the theologian John Hick.[2] Here the key word or image is *soul-making*. We are to think of ourselves not as once perfect beings who have fallen disastrously away from what God intended us to be, but as the raw material out of which people have still to be created or 'made'. The quality of their lives will then reflect the divine life, a life like the life of God, the features of which are revealed to us in Christ. Men and women cannot be forced to achieve and adopt this quality of life. The children of God cannot be manufactured. The creative work is accomplished only by their own free responses to the worldly environment which God has provided for them and which is best suited to the purpose not of giving them undiluted pleasure but of fostering in them such qualities as 'moral integrity, unselfishness, compassion, courage, humour, reverence for truth and perhaps above all the capacity for love'.[3] The process of soul-making is not completed in this world. Other suitable worlds or environments await us; and the end of the story is not the regaining of a paradise once lost but a kingdom yet to come in all its glory.

To take one more example from a modern writer, H. A. Williams tells a story about *resurrection*.[4] We are to think of ourselves as coming to life from the dead. All that is wrong with us and therefore death-dealing is transformed into what is right and life enhancing. What this means is spelt out under five general themes: body, mind, goodness, suffering and death, and any number of concrete examples. The dualism of mind and body in which the body is controlled and even enslaved by the mind so that it has no life of its own gives way to the unity of mind and body and the experience of oneness with myself and the external world. The kind of knowledge which observes, calculates and possesses is transformed into knowledge as communion where the knower is personally involved in what is known. Goodness as conformity to inherited rules becomes a goodness of our own for which we take responsibility. And suffering, instead of threatening to diminish and destroy us, becomes the occasion when we are enlarged and enriched as persons and become more of ourselves. How does resurrection come about? Essentially it is a miracle and we do not know, though it is a miracle that can occur in any of the day-to-day experiences of ordinary men and women where lies the potential creativity of life itself. The result of this miracle, however, also becomes its agent, in that what has been raised to life from the dead itself becomes life-giving. The miracle may bring about new vision of what we are or might be, or the ability to accept and love what we hate about ourselves, or a changed attitude to suffering. The miracle has occurred and yet that vision and that love and that suffering can in their turn become the means by which we become immeasurably more alive than before so that we are raised by them from the dead.

We must avoid criticizing these stories for failing where they have never intended to succeed. It is we who have called them 'stories', not their authors. Eliot and Williams do give some indications that they are offering us comprehensive interpretations of our human experience. Eliot describes the whole world as our hospital. The image appears to be all-embracing. Williams concludes that the reality of resurrection is not far off. It may be indescribable but 'it encompasses us, informing everything we are as the water informs and fills the sea . . . as the Eternal Word continuously takes his world to himself and raises it up to resurrection and life.'5 Resurrection is happening everywhere and all the time. Hick on the other hand is particularly concerned to comment on one aspect of experience, namely the problem of evil, even if in doing so he rightly takes a great deal more of our experience into account. But none of the three may have set out to write a 'story' in our sense of the word, so we shall not be concerned to adjudicate between them or assess them on that basis. Instead we shall use them to illustrate the kind of work that needs to be done to make up a good story for ourselves which does not ignore the complexities of theology, represented in this instance by the many and varied doctrines of the faith, and yet offers us a reasonably practical way of bringing them into the reckoning when we reflect on practice.

Paradoxically the best start to making up a story may be to begin with the one we've got! It may be the one we've been telling ourselves and living by for a long time which others may help us to recognize as we reveal it in what we say and do. It may be told by someone else but appeals to us as a way of conceiving our lives which we could readily adopt. Any one of our three examples, about healing, soul-making and resurrection, could easily fall into that category.

Having got our stories, we need first to compare them with others, second to see what account they have taken of Christian doctrine and third to confront them with our experience. These are not of course disciplines we shall pursue all at once or only once, any more than we shall always stick to one story. They need rather to be incorporated into the ongoing conversations of the Church so that stories and parts of stories are repeatedly being confessed and revised and made more adequate.

We must first of all compare our stories with others if we are going to take seriously the Christian community, one of the hallmarks of a Christian point of view. This will mean swapping stories with fellow members of the same local church as well as with our contemporaries beyond our immediate circles and the great company of believers stretching back to New Testament times.

John Hick shows every sign of having made such comparisons in coming to his own understanding of the world as a vale of soul-making. Most notably he sets his story, which owes much to Irenaeus, alongside one just as deeply entrenched in the Christian tradition and owing much to the work of Augustine. Incidentally Hick calls it a 'myth', and what he has to say about a myth is reminiscent of some of the things we have said about a story: 'The great creation-fall-redemption myth has . . . brought within the scope of the simplest human soul a pictorial grasp of the universal significance of the life and death of Jesus.'[6] The Augustinian story is well known. It pictures the first man and woman in an idyllic state until, tempted by Satan, they disobey God and fall into sin, all their descendants and all the world sharing the consequences. God in Christ bears the punishment for their sin which God's justice requires so that all who believe can be forgiven. At the last judgement some will enter eternal life and others be condemned to an everlasting living hell. Hick also compares his story with those of the New Testament. Amongst them he finds one which, like his, understands man's life as a process of personal growth, 'until we all attain . . . to mature manhood, to the measure of the stature of the fullness of Christ' (Eph. 4.13).

When we compare our story with others we may find that they agree so that our story is confirmed, or that other stories complement ours without denying what it has to say, or there may be outright disagreement. All the stories we outlined agree that our suffering whatever its negative qualities can be turned to our good. Eliot confesses: 'Our only health is disease'. Hick and Williams go into more detail. One believes that the features of the world which give us anything but pleasure can actually contribute to the 'realization of the most valuable potentialities of human personality'. The other believes much the same. The suffering which threatens to destroy us can, if taken on board, be the means by which we discover a larger self with 'resources of strength, and insight and courage and heroism and love and compassion of which so far we have been totally unaware'. Again the creative capacity of which Williams speaks, lying hidden within everything and giving rise to daily miracles, sounds much the same as Hick's belief in the created order's potential for soul-making. It is always capable of stimulating growth. By contrast, if Eliot's poem was intended to be a complete account of the meaning of our lives, then both Hick and Williams disagree with it. The whole earth is not a hospital to make us better. It is an environment in which we can grow up. The whole truth about us is not that we are sick and need to be made well. In some respects it is better than that. We are good raw material being fashioned into the children of God. In some respects it is worse. We are dead and by some miracle need to be made alive. At certain points the stories neither agree nor disagree but complement each other. To mention one, Hick like Williams is well aware that soul-making cannot be guaranteed any more than resurrection. He speaks of a hazardous adventure in individual freedom. But Williams reminds us more forcibly than Hick, who as a philosopher makes every effort to fulfil his responsibility and explain as much as he can, that the outcome is finally inexplicable. One is taken, another is left; and we do not know why or how. Part of the process we may begin to understand. Much of it is miraculous.

Having made comparisons, and we notice they will generate critical dialogue capable to some extent of sorting out one story from another, we must, as a second discipline, enquire into how many Christian doctrines a story has taken into account if it claims to be a comprehensive interpretative framework rather than a commentary on only part of our experience. Any thoroughgoing enquiry will in all honesty be very demanding, since in each case it is not just a doctrine, such as the doctrine of man, that must be taken into account, but something of the variety of opinion that every doctrine represents. However any story worthy of its name must at least deal with the main areas to which doctrines refer.

The Augustinian story which Hick rejects on other grounds shows up well in this respect, almost following through in sequence the major doctrines from creation to the last things. Of our three 'prototypes', Eliot's taken by itself would be the least comprehensive. It deals with the mystery of our redemption, our need for healing and how we are made well, but little else. The other two are much more promising. Earlier on we listed the major doctrines as dealing with God, creation, evil and the fall, man, the person and work of Christ, salvation, the Holy Spirit, the Church, the Kingdom and the last things. Hick speaks of God as father nurturing his children and bringing them to glory; of the created order as a suitable environment in which to grow up and, by that same token, as fundamentally good. Evil and the fall are the main preoccupations of his story and how the reality of them may be reconciled to God's love. Man is spoken of as free and rebellious and his destiny as Christlike but as yet not fully revealed. His salvation is from his failure to become what he is capable of becoming as much as from an evil nature; it has as much to do with maturity as with wholeness and health and forgiveness. His ultimate happiness lies beyond death in the Kingdom of God and at the end of a continuing and costly process of sanctification. For an account of human existence which did not set out to promise an all-embracing image, that is not a bad record. Much of Williams's story might be used to fill out the details of Hick's. His idea of resurrection is after all not far removed from that of soul-making, and both writers speak of a creative enterprise. Williams does however have more to say about God as involved in the process rather than as only providing the appropriate conditions for it to happen. In this way he takes account of the doctrine of the Holy Spirit. Neither comments on the Church!, and on the basis of our summary account of their stories they make little reference to the person and work of Christ though he does find a place in both. In Williams for example Christ is the eternal Word who in his own life and death and resurrection reveals what is always true about God's world. He is the exemplification of God's creative activity in human life, and as such, because he absorbs and uses his suffering in such an exemplary way, he not only finds life for himself but makes an exceptional contribution to the raising of all mankind from the dead.

A third discipline we shall need to work at if we are to have a good story to tell is to ask whether we can go on telling it in the light of those very experiences it claims to interpret. The test can be divided into two parts. First, does the story take account of the major areas of our experience? Is it comprehensive in a second sense? Hick would make no such claim, concentrating his attention on our experience of evil not, as he says, on 'the balancing problem of good'; whereas Williams ranges widely over our physical, mental and moral experience as well as our experience of suffering and death. To apply this test carefully we shall need a check-list of the major areas of human experience similar to our list of major Christian doctrines. Second, we must ask whether within any area of human experience the story that is being told rings true. Can we tell it when face to face with the realities of which it speaks, or are we quickly made to feel embarrassed, or reduced to silence? Can we really believe that all suffering can be used to enhance our personal lives however often we insist that the miracle does not always happen? Is there sufficient evidence of the genuine creativity in human existence of which both Hick and Williams speak?

To be fair to them both, there is abundant evidence in these two books that at this point they have been extraordinarily tough with themselves. Hick's story is after all a theodicy, an attempt to reconcile the old old Christian story about the love of God with the terrible evil, rather than the pastoral care, 'That will not leave us, but prevents us everywhere'. It is a rigorous exercise in making sure that any interpretation comes to terms with experience. And the length of his book bears witness to just how difficult an exercise it is. Williams declares over and over again his distrust of theories. He seems to regard them as a way of talking which is easier but unsatisfactory precisely because it has distanced itself from experience. This he refuses to do. He will speak about what he knows and not what he pretends to know and he will do so in concrete terms drawn from particular examples of what has happened in people's lives. The following lines from his chapter on Resurrection and Suffering are typical: 'Let us therefore abandon comprehensive explanatory systems, theodicies, all the dogma and all the weight, in order to examine at first hand our own experience of suffering.'[7] So close does he keep to experience that his interpretations are almost taken by him to be descriptions.[8] That of course would be to go too far. There is no exact empirical fit. But testing stories against experience is very much like correlating faith with facts. It will always go beyond them, but if faith is what we believe about the facts it must be able to take the facts on board and live with them.

We have tried not to make Aunt Sallies of the images of 'healing', 'soul-making' and 'resurrection', setting them up only to knock them down. In many respects they stand up well to criticism, but we have not assumed that they were ever intended to meet our requirements. Had they been candidates and had we applied our tests more thoroughly, some hesitations about them would have emerged alongside their undoubted virtues. Further reflection on experience would have brought home to us how much of life is bound up with structures and institutions, which they hardly mention. Comparison with stories told by Christians less influenced by western intellectual traditions could have reminded us that the fundamental human reality might be the nation or the community or the people rather than the individual soul or person. Both Hick and Williams are well aware of how much we affect other people and how important they are to us and we to them, but they speak primarily in individual terms and their vision is rarely a corporate one of a kingdom where only because we are so related to each other in justice and love can we at last be ourselves. Again comparison with the kind of story told by Teilhard de Chardin in *The Phenomenon of Man,* or closer consideration of the doctrine of creation, might have made us prefer a story about making a universe to one about making souls. Both Hick and Williams could have made replies. If flesh and blood cannot inherit the Kingdom of God, they too can die and be raised to life and take their place in it. Not only the sons of God but all the created order groans and travails and waits for its adoption. It too has a future and not least because we shall go on needing suitable environments in which to make progress. But in the end, in the case of Hick, the impression survives that it is the making of souls that really counts and that the natural and material world is valued for its contribution to that end, not for itself. Williams relies heavily on the insights and categories of psychology, enriching but possibly limiting; and, to raise one further point, stories of 'soul-making' and 'resurrection' breathe a less desperate, less sombre air than Eliot's story and many people's lives, as if for one of these storytellers life had been more fulfilling than for many and the other had experienced resurrection more vividly than most.

Our enthusiasm for any story that survives the kind of disciplined testing we have described must be qualified in a number of ways. First, any such story is bound to be an over-simplification. Any interpretative framework leaves some things out and tends to tidy up the rest. Life cannot be squeezed into a single image however suggestive or open to elaboration it might be. Second, like the doctrines of the Church, a story may win considerable respect especially if we find it on many lips, repeated time and time again; but it must not be given too much respect since at best it is told from something less than a universal point of view, out of limited experience, conditioned by time and place. It is likely, however, that even if our story is over-simple and only relatively true, the choice is not between reflection informed by faith expressed and handled in this form, and reflection that is informed by patiently referring to the Church's huge and varied body of doctrinal teaching, but between reflection informed by something like a story or not informed by faith very much at all. And of these two we know which is preferable.

If no single story will do therefore it is likely that one will have to do for most of the time; which makes it all the more important to recognize that the stories we use to nourish our minds and imaginations and inform our reflection on pastoral care and all aspects of our Christian obedience cannot function alone. They must be undergirded, criticized, toughened by a refusal to deny the complexities encountered in appropriating and expressing Christian faith which lie just beneath their surface. The one and the many, the relative simplicity of image and narrative and the more complex, prosaic and difficult ways of handling faith must be good and constant companions. In a later chapter we shall suggest how this can be achieved in the life of our churches.

In reflection, stories can be related directly to particular cases of pastoral care. If we believe them we believe them about every moment of our lives so that every one of the six case histories with which we began is to be thought of in these terms. The widest framework within which to understand what is happening to the Johns and Peters, Shirleys and Bills, Josephs and Phyllis' of this world, and what in the end is to be achieved and how best we might share with them in achieving it, is encapsulated in words like 'healing' and 'soul-making' and 'resurrection'.

If I were to tell my own story it would be about 'creativity'. God has invited us to co-operate with him in a creative enterprise to fashion out of the raw material about us and within us a Christlike Kingdom or a new creation. Like all creative enterprises it is achieved only by artists becoming totally committed, absorbed in their work, pouring into it all they have to give and being prepared to run the risks involved. Among them is the risk of making creative and imaginative moves where, by definition, the outcome cannot be calculated in advance and which may turn out to be the wrong moves. One may have been made by God giving us the freedom to do wrong. God, and man, then incur the added cost of redeeming the time, making use of the mistake rather than cancelling it out, incorporating it rather than rejecting it, to enhance the final outcome.

I believe my story can accommodate many of the great Christian doctrines: about man made like a creator in the image of God; about the person and work of Christ as the first-born of the new creation; about incarnation and *kenosis* (becoming totally absorbed and pouring into the enterprise everything you have to give) and redemption; about the misery of man as well as his splendour; about suffering and the glorious end to which the whole creation moves and to which all obedience, with its eschatological dimension, can contribute. My image can carry for me the whole world of Christian doctrine.

It finds it less easy to take account of the full range of human experience, not least the long stretches of uncreative routine that appear to fill so many of our days, and the signs of destruction rather than creativity that are everywhere about us.

Such a story does not have to be related to a situation of pastoral care as if the two were strangers coming upon each other from a distance. Growing out of experience and repeatedly tested against it, the story is like a map of familiar territory on which we locate ourselves, not an abstract theory or conceptual strait-jacket into which we must force our understanding of what is happening to us.

It would be wrong to correlate my story in any serious way with our cases. We do not know enough about them and we are not sufficiently close to those directly involved. But it is not difficult to begin to see how we might talk about them on the story's terms. We should not easily give up the idea that every one of the six situations carries within it not just the possibility of returning to normal, or adjusting to circumstances, or healing old wounds, or doing well along conventional lines, but of moving on and making something fresh and new. Peter and Kate, Bill, Joseph and Gordon, Phyllis and Doris might just be able to see themselves as allies of creative energies at work, part of larger struggles over changing patterns of marriage relationships, sexuality, the place of work, multi-racial communities and attitudes to old age which, where successful, could enhance our life together and build something for the future, and so be inspired to make their own small but courageous experiments as tiny but significant contributions to the whole.

This fundamentally positive vision must not be sunk without trace under the weight of all the negative factors that clamour for our attention. Neither will it turn us into romantics, unaware of the ambiguities which occur at every point and of which our story is quite prepared to speak. What can be thought of as raw material out of which to fashion new kingdoms will also be material going to waste and the toxic waste-product of past mistakes. The tension between Peter and Kate, Shirley's heavy heart, Bill's perplexity, Daniel's bitterness, Doris' disappointment, are not all good potential, grist to the creative mill. The suffering which they all experience in their own way is partly what it costs to achieve anything worthwhile but partly the awful price, multiplying in its effects, that is exacted by false moves. We can neither be totally disapproving of everything they experience as tribulation, nor ever be sanguine about any of it. Our analysis will be more discriminating.

But our story constantly suggests that in addition to the costly self-giving and determination that is required of artists if there is to be any hope of finishing the creative work that is given to us to do, nothing is achieved by trying to be rid of what appears to be the most unpromising features of the scene. The results of the mistakes have to be incorporated in the final design or, to use a by now familiar word in another way, 'accepted' and made use of, not disowned. Nothing is to be gained by trying to deny or defeat or shut away what two young people experience as estrangement, and a widow as fear for her life, and a man as an 'unnatural' passion, and two blacks as injustice, and a middle-aged woman as regret and apprehension. It is by honouring them as useful that they may best be redeemed.

In some such way, by drawing out points of correspondence between case and story, my story may stimulate reflection on my pastoral care. If, however, we are looking for even more realistic and workable strategies for informing our reflection on practice, we may be attracted to a less direct approach. Instead of relating our story to each particular occasion we may relate and integrate it with a consistent approach to caring on all occasions, or to what we shall call our 'pastoral theologies'; and to these we now turn.

Notes

1. John Bowden refers to a 'map' and seems to share some of my concerns: 'The theologian has been portrayed as a cartographer, attempting to draw an outline map of the universe in order to construct an interpretative scheme within which men may plot and make sense of their own thought, actions and experiences.' 'The Future Shape of Popular Theology' in Preston, R. H., ed., *Theology and Change* (SCM Press 1975), pp. 20f.
2. In *Evil and the God of Love* (Collins Fontana 1968), and *Death and Eternal Life* (Collins 1976).
3. *Evil and the God of Love,* op. cit., p. 294.
4. In *True Resurrection,* op. cit.
5. ibid., p. 182.
6. op. cit., pp. 283f.
7. op. cit., p. 142.
8. ibid., p. 34.

SEVEN

Pastoral Theologies

―――――

'Pastoral theology', like 'pastoral care', is a phrase with several meanings. It has been used, along with 'practical theology', to refer to almost all the duties of the clergy from pastoral visiting to conducting rites of passage. Courses in the subject can be so full of hints and helps as to leave little room for theology.

Two other meanings of the phrase come nearer to our concerns. In one the movement is from theology to pastoral practice. We are in a world of 'applied theology'. The relevance of Christian doctrine is exploited. It is used for pastoral purposes. Believing it has things to say about the caring situations which confront us it is now applied to them. Its understanding of human experience is used to explain and evaluate what is going on, and the practical implications of its teaching are drawn out. Faith informs our obedience. Moving in the other direction the experience we gain in pastoral care may inform our faith. Practice may have implications for theology, clarifying what we believe, helping us to appreciate the full force of it, challenging it or producing fresh insights. Daniel William's use of the therapeutic principle of acceptance as a range of comparison with which to expound the doctrine of atonement is an example of this kind of pastoral theology. The vulnerability of our beliefs to the facts would be another. We must take what they say to us into the system. Seward Hiltner set out to produce just such a pastoral theology[1] by allowing the results of his pastoral studies to suggest answers to his theological questions, about the relationship between health and salvation for example, and by building them in as constituent parts of Christian doctrine. A theologian like Eduard Thurneysen would be highly suspicious of these procedures. For him the word of God in Scripture is the only reliable source of truth about man and God. We cannot discover it or reason it out, it needs to be proclaimed to us. We cannot distil it from our own sinful experience, where truth is at best obscured and usually denied. Thurneysen makes it clear[2] that a discipline like psychology is a useful auxiliary science telling us something about the anatomy of the human mind, but we must be careful to dissociate ourselves from its presuppositions about man, and rely solely for understanding on God's revelation in Christ. Our own discussion of the relevance of Christian doctrine was not able to maintain such a sharp division between what we know of God and his purposes through the gospel and what we know of them as we experience and respond to the world about us and within us.

Another meaning of the phrase 'pastoral theology', and the one we shall adopt in the rest of this chapter, is suggested by the way in which 'theology' is often equated with 'theory'. Sometimes there is a pejorative tone about it. Journalists are fond of accusing political parties of indulging in 'theological' debates by which they mean idle theoretical discussions of little practical consequence. Our understanding of a theory will be more closely tied to practice than that. It can be described as a consistent or settled approach to pastoral care, to what it is all about and how it is exercised, which has developed over a period of time through the interplay of growing experience and deep convictions, committed practice and careful reflection. To call it a pastoral theology rather than a plain theory of pastoral care is to suggest that this consistent approach is informed through and through by Christian faith. If so it might offer an even more realistic way of ensuring that our caring draws on the insights of Christian doctrine. They do not even have to be carried about in the convenient form of a 'story', called to mind when we reflect on any particular occasion, since they are already built into the way we habitually go about caring for one another. Where such a theory or pastoral theology exists neither our practice nor our reflection starts from scratch but operates within increasingly familiar guidelines.

The structure of a pastoral theology can be spelt out in a little more detail on the basis of our earlier discussions. It has three levels corresponding to the three basic questions which arise when we reflect on our obedience. There is the level of *analysis* corresponding to the question about the kind of situation we are dealing with and what is really happening. There is the level which deals with our *aims,* corresponding to the question about what we want to achieve; and there is the level which deals with *methods* or how we can move creatively from where we are to where we want to be. At each of these levels our theory or consistent approach to pastoral care will express an opinion. It will be a 'good' opinion because it will have taken notice of all the relevant information it can get from experience and common sense, from the natural and human sciences and related disciplines. It will be a 'Christian' opinion because it will have drawn on the informative resources of faith. It will not only have taken all these voices into account, it will have integrated what they have to say, making sure that facts are checked against facts, and beliefs take facts into account, and assumptions and value judgements and interpretations are seen for what they are and measure up to one another. In addition to that kind of integration where different voices hold appropriate conversations, a pastoral theology will presumably be marked by internal coherence so that what it appears to say at one level is not out of touch or at odds with what it has to say at another.

A Pastoral Theology or Theory of Pastoral Care	
↑ Coherence ↓	Level 1 'analysis' integrating A and B
	Level 2 'aims' integrating A and B
	Level 3 'methods' integrating A and B

A: information which makes for 'good' opinions

B: information which makes for 'Christian' opinions

It would be impossible to conceive of an all-embracing theory somehow taking into account all the areas of human understanding which might offer us insights, and all the caring situations that could come our way. That is just as well; otherwise we might be tempted to think we can tidy up such a highly personal activity as caring for others into a scheme, and become blind to the uniqueness of those who invite us to share a part of their lives, seeing instead only the similarities between one case and the next and always feeling we had been here before. It could make us uncritical and too self-assured at the very point where we need to be reflective. So although we shall strive to achieve for ourselves a consistent approach to pastoral care thoroughly informed by our faith, and are in any case likely to fall into a settled pattern, we shall not complain when any such pattern turns out to be limited. That is how it must be. Instead we shall acknowledge its limitations, recognize what comes within its scope and what does not and try to improve it without ever pretending we can complete it.

Once again it may be best to begin our search for a pastoral theology like our search for a story with one we already have, our own habitual approach or someone else's, and then keep it open to the kind of tests which may from time to time refresh and renew it and occasionally demand its reformulation. Those tests as always include the discipline of comparison, setting any pastoral theology alongside others that have been fashioned by the Christian community and seeing where they correspond or complement each other or disagree. Other tests are suggested by the structure of the theory or pastoral theology itself. Is it coherent? What notice has it taken of other relevant disciplines? What kind of a faith does it imply? Does it comprehend the full range of Christian doctrines adding up to an adequate framework or a story we should want to tell? Finally, has this faith informed the theory in a thoroughgoing way at all three levels, and in an appropriate way, so that it does indeed qualify as a pastoral theology?

Highly developed pastoral theologies appear to be few and far between, but three writers who do not necessarily adopt our use of the phrase, can help us to illustrate some of the points we have just been making. They are Alastair Campbell, Thomas Oden and Frank Lake.[3]

Despite a lengthy warning against falling into stereotyped ways of responding to other people,[4] Campbell sets out for us a consistent approach to pastoral care and one which is highly attractive. It is not tied to the ordained ministry, and it is easy to picture it at work within the kind of settings described at the beginning when we told the stories of Martin, Peter, Shirley, Bill, Joseph and Phyllis. It is a pastoral theology for everyday and everyone and in developing it Campbell is clearly in conversation with the Christian community, comparing his approach to others and rejecting as he does so some of the professionalism and over-dogmatic and judgemental attitudes of the past.

His theory has an obvious limitation, about which we said we have no complaint, in that it concentrates most of its attention on level 3 and in one respect quite deliberately so. Campbell is wary when it comes to level 2 and our aims in pastoral care of going into situations having decided for other people where it is they have to go, which is fair enough provided we realize it does not obviate the need to raise that question with them or encourage them to raise it and tackle it for themselves.

If we ask how we may best care for people the answer is by offering them a certain kind of relationship, and much of Campbell's book is taken up with spelling out just what kind of a relationship it is. It is marked by honesty, steadfastness, personal wholeness, mutuality, the courage of sacrificial love, vulnerability, folly, gracefulness and a companionship which is more like being with people than doing things for them.

Although Campbell believes that 'expertise' can prevent rather than foster this caring relationship, coming between the carer and the cared for, he wishes to avoid blundering incompetence and draws, not uncritically, on secular disciplines, notably those of psychiatry and psychotherapy as represented by Freud and Rogers, Maslow and Erikson. But feeling that these have been over-influential his main interest lies in the direction of Christian faith.

If we try to uncover that faith we find it expressed less in prosaic theological statements or doctrines than in images such as the 'shepherd's courage', the 'wounded healer' and 'wise folly', all of them strongly reminiscent of, even inspired by, Christ, an important resource for reflection we have yet to consider. There is also reference to a story or interpretative framework where life is understood in terms of a *journey* out of the cavern of sin to find a home and companions in God's world and which goes on to discover our personal destination, the true rest for our souls. As we should expect in a limited theory not every aspect of faith is dealt with at equal length. Most attention is given to the doctrine of atonement, which obviously responds to the question about how we help and heal and liberate one another.

Campbell's three images might well qualify as 'ranges of comparison', drawing tightly together what we know to be creative and redemptive in our experience — courage, loyalty, generosity, vulnerability — and what we find exemplified in the living and dying of Jesus. The story of the journey would not do as a comprehensive account of Christian faith or human experience and is typical of the personalism in which pastoral care is so easily trapped. But within its acknowledged limits faith has certainly informed this theory and there are interesting examples of its being integrated with what the psychiatrists and psychologists have to say.

There is for example an interesting if brief encounter between theology and psychotherapy on the subject of sin and guilt. Campbell acknowledges that Freud and Rogers have information which the theologian must take into account when he refers to them as usefully 'clearing the ground' for pastoral care. Freud informs us that much of what we experience as guilt is the result not of outward misdemeanours but inward conflicts provoked by the super-ego, the intro-jected prohibiting voice of our parents. Rogers teaches us that externally imposed values which condition us to feel ashamed of parts of ourselves only result in self-destructive forms of guilt. These observations are of the 'factual' kind though the evidence is less objective than in the case of the natural sciences. Both Freud and Rogers, however, make statements of a quite different kind. Freud believed in the innate destructiveness of man so that without the constraints of the super-ego civilization would break down, and Rogers believed that man was innately reasonable and co-operative so that if the constraints are removed and he is allowed to accept and discover his true self his behaviour, following his impulses, would be positive and constructive. Here, observes Campbell, 'we are encountering two opposing sets of basic assumptions', and he quite properly engages them with the Christian assumptions about hope and about a deeper human tragedy called 'sin' which no individual can remedy out of his own resources. Faith may have to come to terms with facts (clearing the ground) but faith can quarrel with other faiths, and even claim that at certain points it makes more warranted assumptions and takes better account of experience.

In another encounter, this time with Maslow and Erikson, the psychologists describe for the theologian something of the needs of people as they journey through life, but Campbell reminds us again of how, inevitably, such descriptions go beyond the facts and the organization of facts into the realm of faith. 'Theorists like Maslow and Erikson strain psychological categories to breaking point in describing such life searches, because they are trying to describe something beyond psychology—the state of transcendence we call faith.'[5]

Drawing on Christian and secular resources Campbell offers us a pastoral theology which, whilst recognizing its limitations, we might well adopt. If we do we could have a realistic way of ensuring that our pastoral care is constantly informed by our faith because that faith has become an integral part of our consistent approach. But once again such realism will lose its integrity and obscure the difficulties and complexities of any such attempt to integrate theology and practice, if it is not in some way accompanied by the kind of critical questioning we have been trying to illustrate.

Oden's discussion is worth setting alongside Campbell's. Recent approaches to pastoral care have been criticized for being informed by psychotherapy rather than Christian faith, and the psychotherapy has often been that associated with the name of Carl Rogers and his notion of an accepting relationship. Thus when Campbell reviews the contribution of the American writer Seward Hiltner to pastoral care, and in particular his use of the image of 'shepherding' he is

forced to conclude that in Hiltner the image is little more

than a cipher which gives a religious appearance to
statements about care derived from quite other sources,
notably the faith-statements of Rogerian counselling theory.
A consequence of this is that Hiltner's use of shepherding
offers little or no illumination into how we can be shepherds
to one another on that dangerous route which results from
following Jesus.[6]

In which case we have a consistent approach to pastoral care,
entering as fully as possible into another person's world and
their suffering, sharing in their struggles to understand
themselves, accepting without judgement what we find, and
prizing with 'unconditional positive regard' every aspect of
the person that emerges; but we do not have a pastoral
theology.

At first sight Oden seems to invite us to think otherwise,
for he devotes a whole chapter of his book to 'The Theology
of Carl Rogers' and indicates that it clearly has something to
say on levels 1, 2 and 3 in response to all three of our basic
questions. In fact the chapter is divided into three main
sections which deal first with an analysis of man as a gifted
and fallen creature, second with the saving event which
opens up the possibility of self-fulfilment and third with
growth towards the goal of authenticity or the self-accepting
fully-functioning person. The theology appears to inform every
level of the theory and at every point Oden, though not
Rogers, links it with a vocabulary normally associated with
Christian doctrine, so that Rogers can be said to have a
doctrine of man made in the image of God with his innate
tendency to value what is constructive and fulfilling, a
doctrine of sin and the fall, of conversion, growth in grace
and perfection; whilst the accepting relationship is spoken of
as a saving event mediated by anyone who will engage in 'a
certain kind of descent into hell, the hell of the internal
conflict of the estranged man, a kenosis, an incarnate
participation in the suffering of his human brother'.[7]

It begins to sound as if any approach to pastoral care
inspired by Rogers is profoundly informed by Christian faith
and qualifies after all as a 'pastoral theology'.

All is not however as it seems and Oden provides us with a
good example of how important it is, not to insist that a

phrase like 'pastoral theology' must have a single correct meaning, but to make sure that we know what it does mean on any particular occasion. On this occasion it turns out that the 'theology' of Carl Rogers is not Christian faith but more like what Campbell describes as 'the faith-statements of Rogerian counselling theory'. If, says Oden, 'we mean by *theology* a deliberate and systematic attempt to speak self-consistently of man's predicament, redemption and authenticity, then the therapeutic work of Carl Rogers has deep theological concerns, even though he has little to say formally about God'.[8] On this reckoning Rogers 'theology' is no more theological than the assumptions which are part and parcel of most people's statements and on closer examination it is contrary to Christian faith and falls short of it in a number of respects, as Oden and Campbell and others have pointed out. If Rogers has a 'demythologized' or secular doctrine of sin, for example, he has nothing to say about its more tragic, intractable dimension which 'self-actualizing' people cannot cope with out of their own resources and which may force us to provide something more than freedom of expression in an imperfect world. That no doubt is one reason why, if he has a doctrine of redemption, he seems to be unaware of its costly, sacrificial dimensions, where understanding is not enough. And once again we are confronted with a vision which is narrowly individualistic and leaves almost wholly out of account the reconciliation of human society and the destiny of the whole created order. Most fundamentally, the fact that we have a theology without God suggests that if this psychotherapist has gone beyond the facts he has not gone far enough for Christian faith. Oden confirms this. He believes that Rogers has no ultimate justification or grounding for the accepting relationship he so enthusiastically recommends. He cannot finally make sense of it; whereas Oden as a Christian believes he can, grounding it in the forgiveness and love of God demonstrated in the cross of Christ.

Carl Rogers' theology is not a form of Christian faith and his consistent approach to pastoral care is not a pastoral theology. This is no criticism of Rogers as such, only of those who may think that if they have incorporated his insights into their pastoral care it is thereby informed by Christian faith.

Two slight qualifications should be made to this conclusion.

The first is that some Rogerian faith-statements are perfectly compatible with what Christians believe, and that is a useful reminder that Christian convictions are not necessarily different from everybody else's and that they can co-operate in many areas with those with whom they ultimately disagree. Second, although Carl Rogers' theology is not a form of Christian faith and he would probably deny any conscious connection, it remains true as he himself reminds us[9] that he was brought up as a Christian and seriously considered entering the Christian ministry. His views may therefore owe something to Christianity and remind us of the 'formative' link between faith and practice which we have yet to consider.

In 1966 Frank Lake produced a massive volume which promised to set out a scheme of pastoral care integrating psychiatry with Christian theology. If the promise had been kept the result would have been a limited theory as all theories must be, concentrating on severe cases of depression, so that not all that many characters in our stories would have benefited from it, and drawing on only one discipline other than theology. But within those limits it would have qualified as a 'pastoral theology' of the type we have been discussing.

On the psychiatric side it traced the roots of depression to the very first year of life (and even before that to the traumas of birth) when the child did not have enough of its mother's or father's company to give it what we might call a sense of identity but which he calls a sense of being or existing as a person, and when that company, even where it existed, was not sufficiently warm and generous to give the child a sense of well-being. Lacking these gifts the child never grew confident enough to be outgoing and independent, or feel sufficiently cared for to care for others and form good personal relations of its own. Instead anxiety and anger arise over what has been denied, and rage at those who have denied it, together with a lasting sense of unimportance, the attempt to find substitute objects of affection, and the ruthless shutting away of mental pain so that in severe cases one part of the self is split away from another ('the schizoid position'). In later life such deprivation leads to extreme reactions to the strained or broken relationships which more fortunate people take in their stride; and the gracious way in which being secure in the love of others provides a springboard for personal achievement is replaced by the feeling that we must be achievers and win approval if we are ever going to be loved.

Therapy involves uncovering the sad story of these inadequate early relationships which sowed the seeds of depression. Sometimes this is done with the help of drugs but the all-important factor is the understanding, non-judgemental and reassuring attitude of the therapist supplying the courage to face up to the painful experiences which have so far been banned from consciousness.

One test of a theory of pastoral theology involves assessing the contribution of non-theological informants without whom it may be 'Christian' but it cannot be 'good'. In this case that means careful criticism of the kind of psychoanalysis and psychotherapy we can only outline here in a brief and amateurish way. Lake regards much of it as standard stuff but acknowledges that there are other approaches; and he has not, as we would expect, been without his professional critics.

On the theological side a strong appeal is made to the gospel of justification by faith. The depressed person's rage may or may not be justified but he feels guilty over his hostility towards those who wronged him and is convinced that only by his own efforts will he now win acceptance. The cross of Christ teaches him otherwise. If he will turn to Christ instead of false substitutes for the love he has been denied he will be given the status as a child of God which he can never earn, and enjoy the secure and sustaining relationship he was previously denied with its life-giving power to heal him. Loved himself he will be free to love.

This theological ingredient will need testing to see whether it reflects an acceptable framework within which to understand our experience and a sufficiently comprehensive account of Christian doctrine. Taken by itself it will probably be judged as rather narrow since its centre of interest lies with areas of teaching that deal only with small-scale, personal relationships.

Frank Lake explicitly claims to have achieved the integration required of any pastoral theology so that psychiatry and Christian faith inform each other in appropriate ways at the level of analysis (1) and of goals (2) and of moving creatively from one to the other (3). It is possible, however, to come away with the impression that they do not go hand in hand very much at all[10] but follow one after the other so that psychiatry and psychotherapy take us so far and theology and the gospel the rest of the way. Indeed Lake himself can be quoted in support of that view of things. The therapeutic contribution is described as a *preparatio evangelica* (preparing for the gospel) after which

> A transition may now take place, out of the region of psychopathology and the compulsions which savour of determination, into the region of spirituality and the atmosphere of freedom and initiative, in fact of God's intervention . . .

> There is a leap here from comprehensible mental mechanisms to the mystery of God's action in Christ and the recurrent miracle of the Holy Spirit's indwelling and pervasion of the human spirit.

> This is no syllogistic method. 'One, two, three, four, five and there! You are no longer depressed!' The cure of depression by Christian counselling is to call for a miracle in the spiritual order.[11]

All this savours of just the kind of religion of which he disapproves: 'an otherness which does not fit into the context of life'.

But it would be grossly unfair to leave it at that for there is another prominent theological element in Lake's pastoral theology, more obviously though not altogether satisfactorily related to his psychiatry. The fact that it does not tie in completely with his view of the gospel carrying on where psychotherapy stops suggests that his overall thinking lacks inner coherence, though his somewhat haphazard way of presenting material does not always help in fitting the pieces of the jigsaw together.

Lake has a great deal to say about Jesus Christ. For the Christian he is the truth about everything which interests the psychiatrist. He represents the norm of humanity, not the average man but what man is intended to be. He enjoys those crucial relationships with his good mother Mary and with his heavenly Father which gave him his sense of identity or 'being' as a Son and a child of God and fill him with the Spirit of 'well-being' so that he copes with life's difficulties, loves as he is loved, and finishes the work God has given him to do. So it is Christ who informs the therapist of his goals (level 2). He would never discover them from his endless observations of sick and sinful men and women which only yield variations on the theme of their despair.

This same Jesus offers the psychiatrist a true diagnosis of the human condition (level 1). More precisely he offers psychoanalysis a true hypothesis on which to base its account of the origins of depression. The Freudian account, speaking of frustrated primitive appetites, is replaced in favour of explanations which speak of inadequate human relationships denying the infant the companionship and love it needs for healthy and happy development. It is not absolutely clear whether Lake really wishes to say that such notions first occurred to him only when he studied the life of Christ, but he gives that impression. Christ then is the source of a model which best organizes the psychiatric 'facts' uncovered as the patient remembers the first year of life.

Finally, Jesus Christ is the truth about our deliverance (level 3), unlike all the false substitutes we turn to for the love we have been denied. Looking at his cross we see how he has undergone all the deprivations that give rise to our own anguish. He was forsaken by his friends and robbed of all supportive relationships. He was also on the receiving end of our anger hurled at him on our behalf as it were by those who mocked and abused him. There is nothing he does not understand for there is nothing he has not experienced. He is the empathetic listener par excellence, everything that the therapist should be. All the anger that has been hidden away can be shared with him, and we are reassured by his words on the cross, 'Father forgive them for they know not what they do', that we shall not be judged and condemned as a result but accepted. Beyond that is the promise that within the restored relationship with the Father offered by Christ and realized in the fellowship and sacraments of the Church there are powerful resources for dealing with our fear and dread, just as the crucified so plainly had the fortitude to deal with his. Christ becomes a model for the therapist and something of a therapist himself.

In this constant interplay between what the psychiatrist has to say and the word from the cross we sense a greater degree of integration than in the earlier scheme in which the psychiatrist appeared like John the Baptist to prepare the way of the Lord. There must be very real doubts however about the extent to which Frank Lake has actually read off his information from Christ, as he claims to have done, rather than read his own psychiatric and therapeutic theories into Christ, an issue we shall need to pursue as we move on to consider the earthly Jesus as another major resource for our theological reflection on practice. For the moment our aim has been to use the work of Campbell, Oden and Lake to illustrate how faith could conveniently inform practice by being built in to a pastoral theology or habitual approach to caring.

Notes

1. In *Preface to Pastoral Theology,* op. cit. The results are meagre.
2. In *A Theology of Pastoral Care,* op. cit., chapter 10.
3. A. V. Campbell, *Rediscovering Pastoral Care,* op. cit. T. C. Oden, *Kerygma and Counselling.* Westminster 1966. Frank Lake, *Clinical Theology.* Darton, Longman & Todd 1966.
4. op. cit., pp. 104f.
5. op. cit., p. 90.
6. ibid., pp. 32f.
7. op. cit., p. 95.
8. ibid., p. 83.
9. In *On Becoming a Person,* op. cit., chapter 1.
10. One critic accuses Lake of operating 'pastorally with the right hand and theologically with the left'. Graeme Griffin, 'Pastoral Theology and Pastoral Care Overseas', in W. B. Oglesby, ed., *The New Shape of Pastoral Theology* (Abingdon Press 1969), p. 58.
11. Lake, op. cit., pp. 331 and 333.

EIGHT

The Good Shepherd

———

Amidst all the variety of opinion about matters of faith and practice Christians have one thing in common. They all claim to be followers of Jesus and owe allegiance to him as their Lord. Whatever they do or say aspires to be true to him. It seems reasonable to suggest therefore that if pastoral care or any other aspect of our action and reflection is to qualify as Christian it must take him into account at every point. A clear picture of him would seem to be a primary resource which we must draw on if our obedience is to be adequately informed by our faith.

Any serious attempt to do so however bristles with difficulties which have been well rehearsed ever since people became interested in trying to get back behind the layers of tradition about Christ in the quest for the historical Jesus.

One difficulty is that we have very little information to work on, and what we have is all at second hand. We have no writings from Jesus himself, only what others, mainly members of the early Christian churches, have written about him. What they have written is clearly selective, not an exhaustive biography of Jesus;[1] it is coloured by their new-found faith and was set down for other purposes than that of providing a full and accurate account of what he said and did. Added to that we can assume that the evangelists were fallible human beings who, with the best will in the world, didn't always get things right; and even the Gospels admit that Jesus' teaching was frequently misunderstood. To conclude from this that we can know nothing with any confidence about the earthly Jesus who grew up in Nazareth, exercised a short but memorable ministry in Galilee and Judaea and was executed at a comparatively early age by the Roman authorities is generally thought to be unjustified scepticism, but it remains difficult to sort out a picture of

Jesus as he really was from the pictures that were soon being painted of him by his devoted followers.

A second difficulty is the tendency to make Jesus in our own image. When we claim that we have discovered what he was 'really like' he turns out to be remarkably like ourselves, so that we are left with a number of pictures of the real Jesus ranging from the gentle and pallid to the tough revolutionary. It is extraordinarily hard not to see in him what we expect to see or what we have imposed upon him rather than what we have genuinely discovered.

For example, in reacting against the tendency to reduce the criteria for pastoral care to those of the psychotherapist, and in an attempt to restore to it a theological dimension, Alistair Campbell appeals amongst other things to what we know about Jesus as exemplifying and justifying the kind of approach he has in mind. Jesus is the 'courageous shepherd', the 'wounded healer' and the 'fool', and we should be like him. Jesus has become the criterion of this particular outworking of Christian faith and practice. But at several points in the argument we are reminded of just how meagre the evidence can be (our first difficulty) and of how easily we read into it more than is there (our second difficulty). In his discussion of Jesus as the fool or clown, an image recaptured to some extent in the musical *Godspell,* Campbell suggests that '*Godspell* succeeds in restoring the humour and gaiety in the life of Jesus, which (in view of the criticisms made by the religious authorities of his time) must have been present but was quickly lost in the solemnity of pious memories.'[2] In so doing he virtually admits that the evidence is lacking by saying that it was 'lost'. A decision has been made on some other grounds that Jesus was a humorous, musical-comedy type of figure. Later on Campbell suggests that Jesus' treatment of Zacchaeus, inviting himself to his house, is evidence of his 'simple enjoyment of getting close to a fellow human being who welcomes his company'.[3] The incident may be open to that interpretation but it is not necessarily required of us.

When Campbell discusses the beauty and potentiality of any stage in a person's life from infancy to old age he finds that:

the incident reported in Luke's Gospel of the twelve year old Jesus in discussion with the teachers in the Temple is suggestive of what I mean by gracefulness in age . . . There is an unabashed wisdom in such young children . . . They are not necessarily precocious . . . They are simply not cowed by the adult insistence that they should know their place. (What could possibly be said in response to the calm question: 'Why did you have to look for me? Didn't you know that I had to be in my Father's home?').[4]

Admittedly the text is described as merely 'suggestive' but once again we could be asking it to carry more than the evidence can bear, reading into it modern attitudes to children which may have been quite foreign at the time, rather than reading out of it the standard for gracefulness in childhood.

I refer to Campbell because on the whole I warm to what he has to say and find him engaging seriously with the Jesus of history; so that the warning notes which sound when I read him are all the more salutary and pertinent, as if addressed to myself.

John McNeill provides us with one of the most sustained attempts to provide a picture of the earthly Jesus in a book about pastoral care,[5] and it is interesting to see him unconsciously colouring the evidence to suggest that Jesus not only exercised a ministry to individuals but had a preference for it, a suggestion which accords well with much in the western Protestant tradition. Howard Clinebell manages to turn what many would regard as evidence for a political dimension to the mission of Jesus, dealing with the destiny of a people, into firm support for the pastoral counsellor: 'Parts of the quotation from Isaiah 61 which he [Jesus] chose to describe the nature of his ministry also undergird the importance of the task of pastoral counselling: "To proclaim release for prisoners and recovery of sight for the blind; to let the broken victims go free"' (Luke 4.18).[6]

Frank Lake, however, offers us a far more blatant instance of making Jesus in our own image. He claims that a study of the adult life of Christ as God's 'demonstration man', the norm of what all of us are intended to be, reveals him as one whose relationships with his mother (Mary) and his Father (God) offered the personal sustenance and acceptance which

made possible his own well-being and his outgoing relationships with others. It also reveals him as one who shows 'a
complete mastery of anxiety' yet who, 'in the week of His
Passion bore upon His own Person and in His own Spirit
every form of anxiety known to man or borne by him'.[7]

The evidence for the relationship with his mother turns out
to be the fact (!) that the *kenosis* or 'humbling' of our Lord

> did not include the ultimate kenosis of being born in a
> brothel from a sluttish woman who would bring Him up to
> know the seamy side of infancy. Tradition affirms the
> special holiness and godliness of the Blessed Virgin Mary.
> From this it is not unreasonable to infer that God the
> Father was making provision for His Son's human spirit to
> come to 'being' and 'well-being' by response to a woman
> whose character was like His Own, in loving kindness,
> holiness and graciousness.[8]

The evidence for the relationship with his Father is more
substantial though Lake rather curiously appeals to the
doctrinal material in John's Gospel and speaks not so much
of the historical Jesus as of the Christ who abides in the
Father proceeding 'from the Presence of His Father, full of
grace and truth, deeply conscious of His status as the Son of
God'.[9]

The evidence that Jesus experienced every form of anxiety
and mental pain is his crucifixion which, on the evidence of
the Passion narratives, becomes the focus of our human rage,
hatred and envy and the occasion of his identification with
our emptiness, meaninglessness and dereliction.[10]

A number of Lake's suppositions are not unreasonable but
they are clearly not dictated by the available material as he
claims. We are told little about Jesus' relationship with his
mother and what we are told suggests that it did not always
run so very smoothly. His relationship with God, especially
when discussed in such high doctrinal tones, is a strange
substitute for a relationship with a natural father; and
although Christians have often claimed that Jesus ran the
whole gamut of human experiences, we simply do not know
enough about his interior life, let alone his public one, to
know whether that is true or not. What is all too plain is that
Lake's picture of Jesus is a reproduction of his own theory

that the roots of mental illness and mental health lie in our earliest relationships and is required by his and many other Christians' doctrine that we are redeemed by one for whom our particular hell no longer holds any secrets.

It would be unfair and unrealistic to complain unduly about this tendency to make Jesus in our image since the critic will play exactly the same game and we all inevitably apprehend any reality as the people we are. It does mean however that when we refer to our picture of the earthly Jesus as a resource for reflection we may be referring to one that is more like an expression of our faith, epitomized here not in doctrines and stories but an image of Jesus, than an independent yardstick against which we can measure our faith and everything else.

A third difficulty about using the earthly Jesus as a resource has to do with the enormous gap between his world and our own. One indication of how easily we overlook it is the way in which we are struck, say, by the strangeness of the medieval world when we read about it in the history books whereas the world of the New Testament seems quite familiar. The fact that as Christians we know it better because we talk and read about it more often must not obscure the fact that it was a pre-scientific, pre-Freudian, sacralized culture unlike our own. The state of knowledge was different and people grappled with different problems in quite dissimilar circumstances. These discontinuities must make us cautious about assuming that we can ever understand Jesus or that if we did he would have anything relevant to say to us.

Finally, if we believe we can discover something about Jesus' teaching and practice of pastoral care we are left wondering how much notice we should take of it. His genuine humanity opens us to the possibility that as a man of his time his insights are relative and may have been outgrown or be less applicable in a different day and age. His exceptional, not to say divine, stature might on the other hand lead us to the conclusion that patterns of behaviour appropriate to him are not appropriate to us. If he castigates the hypocrites he may be justified in doing so because he alone is in a position to judge, having no beam to remove from his own eye before removing the moat in his brother's. Only if we understand the exceptional stature of Jesus in terms of an exemplification of what human life is like when it has covenanted with God, rather than see it as an essential difference between him and every other human being, can we work with the idea that his caring provides a pattern for our own.

These difficulties add up to an invitation to abandon all attempts to refer to a picture of the earthly Jesus in our theological reflection. We must simply do without what we cannot have. We are left to draw on what Christians, including New Testament Christians, have made of Jesus but with no real dealings with the Jesus of history himself. That may be far from a disastrous situation and it leaves much of our discussion about informing practice with Christian faith intact, which is why, instead of putting first things first as some might wish, we have left our consideration of the historical Jesus so late in the argument. Most will feel, however, that leaving it out altogether would not be the right course to take. It could be said that we have exaggerated some of the difficulties. The picture which Campbell paints of Jesus for instance remains convincing even if some of the details are open to criticism; and maybe Jesus did live in a different world from ours but it seems to be full of the same human emotions and reactions that we know so well. But supposing the difficulties are as great as we have made them out to be, they are still worth living with and indeed ought to be lived with. We cannot ignore Jesus of Nazareth even if he cannot be quite as significant a resource for reflection as we might at first have expected.

If we agree then we are left with our familiar dilemma. We must not over-simplify the issues and pretend the complexities involved in appealing to the earthly Jesus don't exist, but we must not on the other hand end up with disciplines that are far too demanding for most people to cope with. How can realism and integrity co-exist?

We shall adopt an approach to our picture of Jesus that we have used on two previous occasions when we discussed stories and pastoral theologies. We shall begin with the picture we have already got and then try to improve it. It would be well nigh impossible to embark on a personal quest for the historical Jesus. Most of us do not have the technical equipment for the job. But an idea of what Jesus was really like does not lie for any of us at the end of such a long search.

We set out with it from the beginning. We may not spell it out very often but we already have at the back of our minds very definite assumptions about the one we acknowledge as our Lord. The first step towards turning those assumptions into a resource for reflection is to try to uncover them and articulate them in not too defensive a manner.

If we imagine a group of Christians, hardly any of them claiming any expertise as New Testament scholars or technical theologians, it is not hard to stimulate discussion between them in such a way as to make clearer what they believe Jesus was actually like. For example, the question about what he would do in a given situation, like those involving Bill and Shirley and Doris, may seem impossibly naive, especially in the light of the difficulties associated with the distance between Jesus and ourselves which we have just been acknowledging. It may nevertheless be a way of getting at how we think of him. Would he have approved of Martin's single-minded devotion to the Church and told him so rather than encouraging him to be a little more wordly-wise? Would he have advised Shirley to put more trust in God? Would he have shown a deal of sympathy for people like Joseph and Daniel on the margins of society and been highly critical of the powers-that-be but concerned nevertheless to open downcast eyes to alternative sources of wealth and peace of mind and a Kingdom not of this world? Would he have tried to turn Doris away from what in his judgement amounted to self-concern? One can imagine many a Christian making such remarks, and others contradicting them, and so the pictures begin to appear. The Church of course is full of pictures of Jesus. Artists have painted him throughout the Christian centuries. Writers have penned his portrait in words. Plays, films and musicals have been written and performed about him. Some discussion about how a group reacts to any one of these, why they like it or why they don't, will tell us a good deal about the pictures people carry in their heads. Then there are many moments in conversation when a sensitive group leader, or the minister with an eye to the need to raise certain questions in the life of the church, can draw attention to something that has just been said about the proper way to react and ask what it implies about the character of Jesus himself. Equally it is interesting to ask a group to respond rapidly to a list of adjectives lifted straight from the dictionary by asking of each in turn whether it could be ascribed to Jesus or not. Very often those which suggest he could be anything but the nicest possible person to know are quickly scored out! Setting aside all such indirect approaches, people could simply share with one another their own conceptions of the Nazarene.

Having confessed the pictures that already exist we can then proceed to criticize them, chiefly by comparing them with all those other pictures of him that already exist in the Christian community. Some are there within the immediate group or congregation. The most important are in the Gospels and other New Testament writings. As we set them alongside one another, we can look to see where they correspond, complement and contradict each other.

At the very least we may be able to go through one or more of the Gospels and list those passages and incidents which appear to lend support to our account of things and those which do not. Suppose, for the sake of argument, we had uncovered by some means or other a picture of Jesus as the Good Shepherd, endlessly available to people, helping in whatever way he can. Nothing is too much trouble; his door is forever open to the Martins and Peters, Bills and Shirleys of this world so that everyone feels they can go to him with their problems and would willingly do so. He exemplifies all that many would look for in a good pastor.

Leaving on one side what appear to be healing miracles and nothing more (and there are a great many of those) we may be surprised to find that there are relatively few examples in the Gospels of Jesus being involved in pastoral care, understood rather narrowly as dealing with individuals and their problems. They can be counted on the fingers of two hands: the rich young man, the woman or women who washed and anointed the feet of Jesus, Zacchaeus, Martha, the dying thief, Nicodemus, the woman at the well, Thomas, Peter and the woman detected in adultery. Of these, two cases occur after the resurrection and some may find it especially difficult to accept the conversation with the woman at Sychar[11] as anything like a verbatim account of a pastoral encounter. In Matthew Jesus comes over to one reader at least as most certainly a healer, a preacher and a teacher but a pastor hardly at all. A more general reading of the Gospels reveals how Jesus cares for certain groups rather than individuals, such as his disciples, the Pharisees, the general population, sinners and outcasts, the citizens of Jerusalem and the Gentiles. Broad hints may be found in some of the parables like that of the Prodigal Son or Waiting Father,[12] though here as everywhere lurk questions of interpretation. Is the main emphasis on the patience and generous forgiveness of the father (or pastor) or on the pleasure he gets from the homecoming?

Having gone through the Gospels it might be possible to distil out of this material some of the characteristic aims and methods of Jesus' pastoral care, especially if we take the view that even if only a few incidents are recorded they are nevertheless typical of the many. Disciples are in a special category and far more is expected of them than the rest, otherwise his aims are fairly unpretentious. He wants men and women to be sound in wind and limb, well provided for but not over-indulgent, integrated into the community with a modest estimate of their own goodness and a generous attitude towards others. He has a tendency to be unsympathetic towards the self-righteous and impenitent who often feel the lash of his tongue, but he is tender and welcoming towards those whom many others would reject. He seems alert to what is going on in a person's life, aware of the needs of the moment and able to get on to their wave-length. Not beyond parrying a question on occasions he is equally capable of giving a straight answer and is not afraid of issuing clear instructions about what to do. He might even be described at times as being highly directive in his counselling!

But when all this information has been pieced together it may still be difficult to avoid the impression that pastoral care as we have been discussing it is not the main concern of Jesus, or at least that there are other equally important matters on his agenda. They can only be understood as pastoral care in the sense that he is interested in them because of their human consequences and their potential for our good or ill; but it is these larger causes such as his battle over the law, and his struggle with the direction of Jewish history, and the working out of his messianic vocation in relation to the coming Kingdom of God, which lead him inexorably towards acute suffering and death and the climax of his ministry; and it is worth noting that where shepherding is mentioned in so many words it appears to be of a political rather than what we think of as a 'pastoral' kind, where not individuals but the mass of the people is without the leadership it so badly needs, serving the common good.[13]

Without pretending that such efforts to compare the New Testament and other portraits of Jesus with what we have uncovered of our own will resolve entirely any of our difficulties they will alleviate the problem of making Jesus in our own image if only by making us more aware that that is what we and others tend to do. Setting our pictures alongside those from other parts of the world and other periods of Christian history including the very earliest may help us to see how limited and relative and culture-bound our pictures are, and allow one unsatisfactory point of view to criticize and correct another, so that out of the comparative exercise emerges a rather more independent criterion for faith and practice and reference-point for reflection than we would otherwise have had.

What is now to be done with it if it is to inform our pastoral care? I have three suggestions to make. First if we can somehow make disciplines like confessing our pictures of Jesus, criticizing them by comparing them with other pictures, and facing up to them fairly and squarely, actually contemplating them rather than refusing to look at them, part and parcel of the ongoing life of the Church, then the work may already have been done. Actually being involved in such a discipline will imperceptibly shift the way we see things and the way we respond in our caring.

The exercise we have just outlined, jolting some fairly familiar if unsophisticated assumptions about Jesus, is far from complete, but even at this comparatively early stage it may begin to have its effects. It will not, presumably, lead us to despise kindly concern and good neighbourliness. How could they not be part of what it means to love one another? But it may make it less easy for us to equate them with Christian discipleship or the main business of the Church, and it could awaken us to the possibility that following Jesus is a rather more offbeat and strenuous affair, raising issues whose importance is not so widely appreciated and taking action which is not so readily approved of, upsetting as well as consoling, and likely to get people into trouble rather than universally admired. Made less at ease with our previous assumptions we are not quite the same people after we have carried out the exercise as before. The picture of Jesus which has emerged (and which of course will itself be challenged in due course) will inform what we do by forming the men and women who commit themselves to doing it.

Secondly, it will always be worth considering whether there is anything in the teaching of Jesus or his dealings with others or his bearing which is directly related to the issues we are struggling with. Did he at any point talk about the same things, face the same questions, confront much the same kind of people? It is not unproductive to put those questions to our stories about John and Martin, Peter and Daniel and the rest. Widows, outsiders, parents responsible for children, unfulfilled and dissatisfied individuals appear in them, and they cross the path of Jesus. Marriage, family relationships, concern about the future and where the next meal is coming from are talked about in these modern settings and Jesus talked about them with his contemporaries. As to similar questions, maybe it is not just the rich young man in the Gospels who in some sense poses the one about eternal life and who might benefit from disposing of the very thing, not necessarily possessions, that has always been regarded as the key to achieving it. Even Doris might find the suggestion worth considering!

Of course there is an enormous distance between all our characters and Jesus, but to respect an historical figure by taking seriously his opinions and reactions is not to feel you have to take them over. It is rather to engage with them and allow them the right to stimulate your own thinking in an open debate. In the course of it we may find ourselves saying: 'I had never thought of that, or taken it sufficiently into account.' When we do, we have discovered something of value in its own right and it is of secondary importance whether or not it is quite what Jesus would have said or done.

The third suggestion is that even where we don't feel confident about taking a positive lead from our conclusions about Jesus of Nazareth we may at least ask whether what we propose to do after careful reflection could be done in his presence, as it were, without an acute sense of embarrassment? Would it be compatible with our vision of him who is 'Christlike and in whom there is no unChristlikeness at all'? It may be well-nigh impossible to move from his world with detailed implications for ours, but it may be possible with a little imagination to move back from our world into his and see whether such a move creates a critical disturbance where before there seemed to be a perfectly sensible approach to pastoral care, so that we are made to think again even if we are not offered an explicit alternative. Our measured speech for example may be upset by the harshness, even rudeness, of his language; our acceptance by his judgemental attitudes; our preference for listening and saying little by his forthright verbal engagements; our search for fulfilment by his own abrupt end and humiliation; our concern for good relationships by his warning that not a few will be wrecked before the Kingdom comes and his insistence that charity does not always begin at home; our ideal of mature independence by his overdependence on his Father; our tendency to opt for the small-scale and the palliative by his wholesale and radical approach. Any such dissonance which may arise between our methods and aims in pastoral care and what we discover about Jesus of Nazareth may be unnerving and annoying but potentially creative all the same.

Once we move far beyond these three ways of using our pictures of Jesus to inform our pastoral care, we soon discover that we are dealing once again with what we and other Christians have come to believe in the light of Jesus, the doctrines, stories and interpretative frameworks of our faith, rather than with the historical Jesus himself. It is worth noting, however, that if one way of testing out our pastoral care is to imagine whether we might feel comfortable or not practising it in his presence, a way of testing our doctrines and stories and beliefs is to ask not so much whether they are derived from what we know of him but whether once arrived at they are compatible with the picture of Jesus and therefore of Christlikeness we are at present able to paint.

Notes

1. cf. John 21.25.
2. Campbell, op. cit., p. 57.
3. ibid., p. 61.
4. ibid., p. 79.
5. *A History of the Cure of Souls* (Harper and Row 1951), pp. 69—79.
6. *Basic Types of Pastoral Counselling* (Abingdon Press 1966), pp. 47f.
7. Lake, op. cit., pp. 30f.
8. ibid., p. 137.
9. ibid., p. 135.
10. ibid., pp. 190ff.
11. John 4. The same could be said of John 3.1—21.
12. Luke 15.
13. See, for example, Mark 6.34.

NINE

Doing Theology in Community

Building on our discussion in the previous chapters we can now outline a procedure for reflecting on practice, in this case on our practice of pastoral care. We can map out what we should try to do, or a John or a David or a Gordon or Doris or the chaplain should try to do, when the moment comes to stop and think about characters like Martin and Peter, Shirley, Bill, Joseph and Phyllis, sometimes with them and sometimes by ourselves.

1. First, we shall raise our three basic questions about (a) what kind of situation we are dealing with, (b) what we should aim to achieve and (c) how we can move creatively from one to the other (see pages 25—28).

2. Second, we shall ask about the information we need to make 'good' judgements about all three questions, which is not offered to us by Christian faith as such, and set out to obtain it (see chapter 4).

3. Third, remembering that Christian doctrine is often talking directly or indirectly about the very issues we are raising: about the realities of the human situation, about what we are meant to be and become and about how we and all God's creatures are redeemed and brought to glory (see pages 42—49), we shall take those which seem most relevant on this occasion and see what they have to say.

4. Fourth, we shall avoid being over-selective about which doctrines we choose to consider by trying to set our three questions within a comprehensive interpretative framework, or the story we are prepared to tell about our lives, and see how such an expression of our faith would respond to them (see pages 69—72). This may also be a practical way of handling without ignoring the variety and detail of Christian doctrine.

5. Fifth, we shall correlate the insights gained under 2, 3 and 4, remembering each includes a range of factual and interpretative material, and ask where they reinforce each other, where there is legitimate room for disagreement and where one informant needs to take another more seriously into account (see pages 49–56).

6. Sixth, we shall make some provisional judgements in reply to our three basic questions which may then be further checked and reflected on in the following three ways:

7. by asking about their compatibility with the picture we have of the earthly Jesus (see pages 97f);

8. by seeing how far what we propose complies with our pastoral theology or consistent approach to pastoral care, possibly raising questions about that approach as well as about our proposals;

9. by comparing them with the responses of other Christians to similar cases.

10. Finally, we must make our judgements however open they must be to revision in the light of further experience and reflection, and commit ourselves to the next stage of practical obedience.

This procedure assumes at least three ongoing and supportive disciplines. One is the attempt to make up and tell a good story (as described in chapter 6), another is filling out and contemplating a picture of the earthly Jesus (as described in chapter 8), and the third is building and improving a pastoral theology (as described in chapter 7).

The procedure includes two important elements which we have scarcely mentioned so far. The reference under 9 to other known *cases* needs no explaining. Very often it will mean comparing notes in an informal way with Christians who have had similar experiences, though in certain fields (marriage guidance, homosexuality, unemployment, old age would be examples) there will be a body of case histories which, treated with care, could be of great help. On occasions older literature including the Bible will deal with the same issues that we are dealing with and will be worth consulting, though we shall need to remember that changes in culture and circumstances often make the similarities more apparent than real.

The other new element referred to is that of *judgement.* It will have been noticed that throughout this book we have come to few conclusions. We have described several cases of pastoral care when we told stories about Martin, Peter, Shirley, Bill, Joseph and Phyllis but have dealt with none of them. We asked what is meant by pastoral care but remained content with a description of what we were talking about rather than a definition. We mapped out conversations about making up stories or satisfactory interpretations of our human experience, and accounts of the earthly Jesus and theories of pastoral care, but stopped short of stating the outcome. We could be accused of inconsequential chatter and a general unwillingness to come clean.

This failure is partly due to the fact that our main concern is with a method of allowing our faith to inform our practice rather than with the results of actually doing so, and on that we *have* arrived at some conclusions and will arrive at some more in this chapter. The failure is also consistent with our declaration that pastoral care is Christian not because it has arrived at and been true to convictions and followed practices which can be ticked off as 'correct', but because it has arrived at them in an adequate way by taking into account the resources of the Christian theological tradition.

Over and above these considerations, however, is the crucial point that any conclusions we arrive at, in this case about our practice of pastoral care, must be the children of our own responsible judgements. There is no process of reflection which can, if followed step by step, lead us inevitably to the answers to our questions, as if having correctly programmed the theological computer we have only to wait for it to produce the required results. Rather, the process of reflection nourishes our minds and provides them with a far richer store of new material out of which we have to make a judgement and take a decision. It provides food for action and not just for thought, but it will never decide for us what action to take.

Recognizing this we may also be able to guard against the real possibility of Christian thought and practice being over-determined by the past. It is inevitable that if Christian reflection entails taking the resources of the total Christian community into account as best we can it will be almost wholly concerned with the past since the past is all we have. To remind ourselves that when we have paid it our due respects we have still something to add of our own, that we have to make something of it rather than merely comply with it or hand it on, that we have quite literally to 'make' a judgement and 'make up' our minds, is to remind ourselves that there is a creative element in the rhythm of action and reflection which we cannot avoid and for which we have to take responsibility. Any story must in the end be ours, the one we are prepared to tell; any picture of the earthly Jesus must be one which with integrity we feel able to paint and adopt; any pastoral theology must be one we can work with with conviction; any commitments we make as the moment of reflection comes to an end and the practice of pastoral care is taken up again must be matters of obedience for us: what with our limited insight and understanding and therefore a proper measure of scepticism we now know we have to do.

I would expect a procedure somewhat similar to the one we have outlined to be followed whenever we sit down with those with whom we are involved in pastoral care, to think through in a careful and tough-minded way about a pastoral situation. It could also provide a scheme for reflective and meditative prayer in the personal effort to know and to do what we might refer to as 'the will of God'. It nevertheless represents a time-consuming, demanding and complicated enterprise which many Christians on the majority of occasions will feel unable to attempt. It would seem unreasonable and unrealistic to expect them to do so and unwise simply to bemoan the fact that they don't, since the result will not be an improvement but a perpetuation of the divorce between Christian faith and pastoral care that we wish to overcome. Is there then a way of 'doing theology in community' or a pattern of congregational life which might ensure that everyone reflects theologically on practice, if not without knowing it then certainly in a way that makes realistic and not impossible demands on them? Could such a pattern also ensure that the complexities of theology and reflection are not totally denied; and could it go some way to forging a fourth, 'formative' link between our faith and our caring, besides the transformative, supportive and informative ones, so that when people have no time except to 'be themselves' and act 'without thinking' their spontaneous reactions are nevertheless informed by their faith because it has shaped or formed the kind of people they have become?

The type of Christian congregation I have in mind expresses its corporate life in three core activities. If pressed I would find it hard to argue that any additional ones were absolutely essential. They are the Sunday service, the congregational meeting, and the fellowship group. Let us suppose that the first is weekly, the second bi-monthly and the third fortnightly. The Sunday service will be the occasion when all the people gather to read the Scriptures, hear the sermon, say their prayers, share bread and wine and make their offerings through Christ to God. The fellowship group will bring together about a dozen people whose main concern is to focus attention on their Christian practice: the tasks they do together as a group and those they do as individuals in the everyday world. As part of their support for one another they will share their experiences, reflect on them and try to discern what it is that Christian obedience requires. The congregational meeting, about which we need say little, will review and take decisions about the life and work of the whole congregation, reflected in the reports, requests and proposals from the smaller fellowship groups, with a special concern for making available resources where individuals and groups cannot provide for themselves. In addition to these three core activities I assume that the congregation would have available the services of a trained minister appointed to enable the people in appropriate ways to fulfil their corporate and individual vocations.

If Christian obedience in the form of pastoral care is to be informed by Christian faith—and that is the single aspect of this congregation's life we are discussing, though I believe it can be integrated with every other aspect—then on the basis of all that we have said it is absolutely essential that:

A people are committed to practice, in this case the practice of pastoral care, as the only setting in which the kind of reflection we have been talking about is worth our time and effort;

B there is recognition of the need and respect for information which cannot be provided by Christian faith as such, and a convenient way of obtaining it;

C a comprehensive faith in the form of an interpretative framework or story, taking Christian doctrine and experience into account, is constantly articulated and critically reviewed;

D a picture of the earthly Jesus is likewise confessed, confronted and criticized;

E there is access to the Christian tradition to provide material for the kind of comparative work we have constantly seen to be important;

F there is a flow of conversation between all these elements: practical commitments, secular insights, story, picture and tradition, even if it cannot always be as careful as in our more formal procedure for reflection.

Now let us look again at our Christian congregation to see where these essential marks of the Church might appear.

Commitment to practice (*A*) is the assumption behind the fellowship groups with their focus on tasks. Fellowship is understood not as meeting for the sake of meeting or only to generate and deepen relationships but as partnership in the work of the gospel. Though few will escape some involvement, not everyone or every group will see the work of pastoral care as the main concern. Some, for example, may be more concerned about evangelism or social action. Where the emphasis is on pastoral care, the group may be together in caring for old people or the unemployed or the handicapped or particular cases of need but it will also be together in taking seriously the pastoral responsibilities which every member has to shoulder at home, at work and in the community as part of the substance of their Christian obedience. We can imagine for instance that Phyllis might well come on to a group's agenda as a result of its own organized caring activities but that John encountered Martin and the chaplain encountered Bill in the course of their daily work. Commitment will also find expression in the Sunday service. Rather like reflection is to practice so worship may be understood as a momentary pause in the ongoing mission of the Church, concluding on a characteristically dismissive note as the congregation is sent away to resume their work with God in his world. Even within the service itself commitment to practice will be expressed at the intercessions where the level of caring for others with God affirmed in prayer can be no higher than the level of caring exercised by the group and its members from day to day.

Access to a considerable amount of the information which makes for 'good' and well-informed decisions (B) will be available if the knowledge, training and experience of the laity is fully researched and honoured, so that the congregation is aware of it, and makes use of it. It can be supplemented where necessary by an enabling minister or leader who has taken the trouble to find out where there are well-informed and qualified people and organizations in the neighbourhood or wider denominational and ecumenical circles who are willing to help.

Few will be surprised if members of the fellowship groups are encouraged to talk together about their faith (C). In many people's minds that is what house groups in the church are usually for. Discussion starters are many and varied, including Bible study, Sunday's sermon, an area of Christian teaching highlighted at that particular time of year, a book, a controversy, a genuine difficulty, a personal testimony. As people react and exchange views, fragments of their own stories, or what they believe about their life in God's world, will emerge. These stories will be continually criticized in a constructive way by testing them against experience and by comparing them within the group and with the confessions of faith of other Christians and the historic faiths and doctrines of the Church.

It may well be possible from time to time to persuade people to tell stories about their lives, about growing up and healing and creativity and journeying, about playing a game or fighting a battle, about searching and struggling or however they imagine it, and seeing which particular image or metaphor is most satisfying as the story of all the other lives they know and is best able to take account of the full range of Christian teaching and human experience. But if discussing the faith is a fairly familiar group activity, here it will not stop at a piece of Christian education or a good argument however valuable, but be firmly wedded to the desire to respond adequately to the tasks of Christian discipleship.

Pictures of the earthly Jesus (*D*) against which all Christian practice must be tested, can also be explored within the small group. Simple discussion starters again include Bible study as well as actual pictures of Jesus to which people are invited to react positively or negatively and explain why, or recent accounts of him in books or films or plays, or the not too cautious attempt to say what he might have done in a given situation. The criticism of these pictures which respects the complexity underlying any attempt to recover the historical Jesus can proceed by the group exploring its own individual agreements and disagreements, by comparing its ideas with those of other parts of the Church and above all by referring to the Gospels. At the very least we can ask which gospel passages appear to lend support to our view and which raise questions about it.

The enabling minister or leader will have several important tasks. One is to see that these essential matters are discussed and that fragments of stories and pictures are put together and given back to a group as some sort of coherent whole. Another, and perhaps the most distinctive, is to see that the resources (*E*) are available for a fruitful discussion. It is not a minister's business to dictate what the picture or the story should be, since no single one is correct and the minister is not necessarily the best judge of which one should be adopted by any particular person or group. Part of the meaning of ordination, however, is that the Church recognizes the minister as one who is familiar with the Christian tradition, what it comprises and how its catholic wealth can be dug out and made available to the local congregation. He can make available something of the wide range of the Church's pictures and stories. He can recount what the Church has believed from time to time and how it has conceived of and understood its Lord. He can make sure that there is plenty of material with which his congregation can compare their own ideas. It is not his calling to say exactly what they should make of it all, but it is his calling to put it in their hands to use. This is his special competence helping to inform the congregation in a way which is different but complementary to the equally important information provided by the laity.

The story (*C*) and the picture (*D*) will also feature
prominently in the Sunday service. The whole liturgy evokes
pictures of Jesus as it constantly 'remembers' him by reading
from the Gospels, following the saga of his life and death and
resurrection during the course of the Christian Year, and
giving thanks for his sacrifice and his living presence in the
breaking and sharing of the eucharistic feast. The faith of the
Church or the story it has to tell or the interpretation it has to
offer of our experience in the world is also rehearsed in
biblical words, in psalm and creed and hymn and testimony.
The main business of preaching could be said to be not
chastizing the congregation for its failures or fruitlessly
exhorting it to even greater endeavour but drawing attention
to Jesus the Lord and articulating the faith of this believing
community at this moment in its pilgrimage. The emphasis
now is not on discussion and criticism but on proclamation.

Once again the enabling minister has a distinctive but
limited role to play. He will not decide in isolation what that
proclamation is to be. He is not the judge of it except to
ensure that it is always open to the judgement of the wider
witness of the Church. He will rather listen carefully to the
pictures and stories confessed and critically examined in the
fellowship groups and in his private conversations, test out
what he might say with people before he preaches it and,
gathering up this material, re-present it to the congregation in
the liturgical proclamation, confronting them with their Lord,
not just his, and reshaping them according to their own faith.

The Sunday service is probably not the place where the
vital conversation (*F*) takes place, though the liturgy will
faithfully juxtapose many of the voices which need to be
heard. The practical commitments of the people (*A*) will be
assumed and reflected in their acts of dedication, their
intercessions and the dismissal at the close of the service.
The honouring of their skills and secular understanding (*B*)
will be part of the total offering of life to God. The story or
believing framework which is their faith (*C*) and their picture
of Jesus (*D*) will be rehearsed. Worship will rejoice in the
devotional riches of the catholic Church (*E*) rather than be
impoverished by a narrow parochialism. Prophetic preaching
which tries to articulate the good news of God about particular
moments of our lives, including moments of pastoral care,

will only arise out of a vigorous encounter (*F*) between many of these elements.

But the fellowship group, not the liturgy, is the more obvious place to talk. At a typical meeting conversation could, for example, follow roughly the procedure we have outlined for reflecting on practice, beginning with the precise details of a situation of pastoral care and the questions which it raises, and leading on to some discussion of the faith which informs the practice and to judgements about where obedience lies. But let us try to be more imaginative, casting the fellowship group's meeting into something like the shape of the liturgy or great Sunday service of word and sacrament, but done here in informal rather than formal style.

The group is one of a number associated with a church in a large industrial conurbation. It is not itself in the inner city and most of its members do not live there though they are not completely untouched by its problems. Doris, who knows that very well through her contacts with Phyllis, is a very active churchgoer and host for the evening. Her husband is not as active in the church as she is and sometimes resents the amount of time Doris is out and about at meetings and visiting mainly old people. This evening he is out in any case.

People arrive from seven o'clock onwards, each of them bringing a modest contribution to supper. Since most have belonged to the group for over a year now there is no shortage of friendly greetings and general conversation as they catch up on one another's news. Margaret the minister is there. She also acts as a part-time chaplain to students at the local university. David is there with his wife Susan. Shirley is one of the last to arrive after organizing the boys' tea and homework before rushing out. By half past seven all eleven group members have arrived. Not everyone in the church is involved in a group of this kind but those who are are regular in attendance.

As usual, the host leads a short prayer and organizes the reading of the three lectionary passages (Old Testament, Epistle and Gospel) listed for next Sunday. She also comments briefly on one of them. Doris chooses to talk about the passage from John's Gospel about the light of the world because she's particularly fond of it, and she has brought a small postcard-sized reproduction of Holman Hunt's famous picture to show the group. At least one person suppresses the desire to tell her how much he dislikes it.

Everyone then joins in a brief affirmation of faith which the group has been working on over the past few months and felt able to make its own. It relies heavily on an image taken from W. H. Vanstone's *Love's Endeavour Love's Expense*[1] which impressed them greatly when they studied parts of it together. It speaks with great subtlety of the creative activity of God, disclosed in Christ, who like an artist expends in love all the resources he can command to discover the possibilities that lie within the form he has chosen to work with, overcoming the unforeseeable problems, redeeming the steps that prove to be false, risking the tragic possibility that his love once lavished will not receive a response, but never abandoning his work whilst the vision which is only discovered in the endeavour remains unrealized. Doris' group has increasingly found in this imagery, firmly linked to but casting fresh light on more traditional Christian teaching, a fruitful way of interpreting their human experience as creatures actively caught up and sharing in the creative enterprise. (Picture and story are already making their presence felt.)

Supper follows these devotions and over it a lot of relaxed but disciplined conversation. The group knows it is there for a purpose. It has particular responsibility for the care of older people in the area and everyone is given the opportunity and in a way is expected to talk about what they have been doing since the last meeting.

Doris, aware that she must be careful not to hog the conversation, is particularly keen to talk about Phyllis. She has been to see her twice. She is convinced she can't be left to live alone much longer and she can't stop thinking about what Phyllis might have been and done in life if only she'd had the chance. It all seems such a waste. The group by now has good contacts with the social services and Doris is reminded that she needs to check on what is happening in that direction, and since a number of people present have elderly friends or relatives who want to keep their independence but can't really manage on their own it is generally agreed that they ought as a group to get someone with experience to give them a bit of advice and look more carefully at what facilities are available or are needed. There is also considerable discussion, partly initiated by Margaret, about recognizing and living with limitations as well as creative possibilities, and how that could save us from unrealism and frustration without becoming an excuse for lowering our sights when we should be raising them. Someone in the group comments that the 'Light of the world' had made a blind man see. There seemed to be no limit to what he could do. Others remember that Vanstone was not unaware of the issue they were struggling with and allowed for it in his story.

The conversation is not all about the elderly. David has met up with an old college friend whose marriage is in difficulties. Margaret is sure that she should not mention Bill by name as he had talked to her in confidence about his homosexuality, but reports that the issue of homosexuality, especially Christianity and homosexuality, is very much on her mind and that she feels the need to test out what some might regard as her own rather relaxed views on the subject with those who might take a more conservative approach. Shirley takes her up and is fairly hostile.

After a good hour of conversation, not much of it conclusive, just before nine o'clock, Susan agrees to lead the intercessions. Forewarned, she has kept a note of the people and the issues that have been mentioned during the course of the evening and invites the group to pray about each one in turn. Often this is done in silence. Sometimes someone prays out loud. The words, 'Father this is our prayer', said by Susan followed by 'Help us to know and to do your will', said by everyone, effect the transition from one topic to another. After the prayers the group shares the peace. They have grown used to either clasping hands or embracing. Shirley thinks she'd better make a special effort to have a word with Margaret! Hands joined, the grace is said.

The last quarter of an hour is taken up with the familiar actions of the communion service: offering, thanking, breaking and sharing. The offering includes setting aside some of the bread and wine that has been brought for supper and a moment when one or two people share with the rest lines of action or lines of thought which they are now committed to following through. Margaret has picked up a theme for Sunday's sermon. The thanksgiving has been written out and is said responsively but it allows for spontaneous expressions of gratitude, some of which reflect the evening's discussion and the Bible readings. After passing round and sharing bread and wine, an evening prayer is said, the host greets her guests: 'The Lord be with you', and they reply 'And also with you', and there is a sense of 'back to work'.

Some of the group have to get away quickly. Others, including Shirley, stay to talk. David asks her about the boys and how things are going and she always finds him a good listener. Doris' husband eventually walks in, managing a smile. 'Still at it then?', he asks.

Any single meeting of a fellowship group along the lines described, and however idealized, may be better than nothing but will not of course achieve the kind of interchange and integration of pastoral care and Christian faith we are searching for. What is talked about is inevitably haphazard and disjointed. Stories and pictures are not fashioned in an evening. Not every topic can be pursued in a rounded or exhaustive way. In any case the group needs the constant input of experience and the constant rhythm of action and reflection. Only over a period of time will resources be built up and a settled and consistent way of doing things emerge informed by Christian faith, and the group develop, almost without noticing it, a 'pastoral theology'.

The enabling minister, sharing in the life of these groups and other congregational meetings, will be less concerned with the outcome of these conversations than to ensure that they take place and that the many varied voices $(A-E)$ have a chance to be heard. This may leave him with the responsibility (which Margaret accepted at one point) of seeing that certain questions are put, such as how the way we are perceiving a set of circumstances and what we are proposing to do about it relates to our faith and whether it is at least compatible with following Christ. He may creatively evoke the whole 'theological underworld' of the group's life by asking naively, 'What would Jesus do?', or whether we 'believe in what we are doing'. From time to time he will need to help the group uncover and articulate not only its assumptions about Jesus and its faith but its 'pastoral theology', and then to examine and revise it along lines similar to those discussed in chapter 7.

This pattern of congregational life with its Sunday service, fellowship groups, congregational meetings and enabling minister has many familiar ingredients if not familiar emphases. It makes sure that people talk about their faith, study the Bible and the Church's teaching, share in worship, share their experiences and responsibilities, pool their expertise, help one another to be obedient. It is less concerned about the institution for its own sake and more concerned about how it helps and supports Christian discipleship. It understands the complementary role of the ordained and other ministries. It takes seriously the extramural life of the Church. It sees itself in the business of believing and reflecting far more than many congregations do. I believe that where an enabling minister makes a proper contribution, ensuring that disciplines are followed, questions are asked, connections attempted and adequate resources are to hand, this pattern makes realistic demands of people and provides adequate opportunities for faith to inform practice; and there is a very real sense in which, by living in it and being part of it, Christians will be formed as theologians. For one thing they are so repeatedly exposed to a process of sharing, rethinking and affirming the faith by which they live and the character of him they name as Lord that pictures and stories become part of the 'ingrained' way they respond to situations of pastoral care. Their pastoral theology becomes a living part of themselves quite apart from any deliberate attempt to integrate faith and practice on any particular occasion. In addition members of the congregation who might shrink from any idea of reflecting theologically on practice grow accustomed to a certain way of doing things, of moving between what they practice and what they believe and struggling to make connections. They are forced not only to act spontaneously in ways that are informed by faith when there is little time to reflect; but to assume that when there is time and when they make time, shared conversations with other Christians which draw amongst other things on the rich resources of many Christian traditions are the normal way to discern what it is they now have to do. Men and women become theologians, laying hold of and using theological resources by being part of the ongoing life of a community and a continuous process of theological education. The duly appointed (or ordained) enabling minister when acting as a theologian in a special sense, neither denies nor offers a pale repeat performance of the scholars' role but takes the fruit of their work and makes it available to nourish the life of the local congregation and provide it with some of the essential raw material out of which Christian decisions and commitments are made. This 'theological' community may incidentally also be a profoundly 'pastoral' community. By forming its people for caring it may offer to them themselves one of the best and most respectful forms of pastoral care.

Notes

1. Darton, Longman & Todd 1977, see especially pp. 58–70.

Select Bibliography

Campbell, A. V., *Rediscovering Pastoral Care*. Darton, Longman & Todd 1981.

Clebsch, W. A., and Jaekle, C. R., *Pastoral Care in Historical Perspective*. Jason Aronson 1975.

Clinebell, Howard J., *Basic Types of Pastoral Counseling*. Abingdon Press 1966.

Cobb, John B., *Theology and Pastoral Care*. Fortress Press 1977.

Dillistone, F. W., *The Christian Understanding of Atonement*. Nisbet 1968.

Halmos, Paul, *The Faith of the Counsellors*. Constable 1965.

Heywood, Jean, *Casework and Pastoral Care*. SPCK 1967.

Hick, John, *Evil and the God of Love*. Collins Fontana 1968.

Hiltner, Seward, *Preface to Pastoral Theology*. Abingdon Press 1958.

Jacobs, Michael, *Still Small Voice*. SPCK 1982.

Lake, Frank, *Clinical Theology*. Darton, Longman & Todd 1966.

Lee, R. S., *Principles of Pastoral Counselling*. SPCK 1980.

Leech, Kenneth, *Pastoral Care and the Drug Scene*. SPCK 1970.

McNeill, John T., *A History of the Cure of Souls*. Harper & Row 1951.

Oden, T. C., *Kerygma and Counselling*. Westminster 1966.

Oglesby, W. B., ed., *The New Shape of Pastoral Theology*. Abingdon Press 1969.

Rogers, Carl R., *On Becoming a Person*. Constable 1977.

Thurneysen, Eduard, *A Theology of Pastoral Care*. John Knox Press 1963.

Vanstone, W. H., *Love's Endeavour Love's Expense*. Darton, Longman & Todd 1977.

Williams, Daniel Day, *The Minister and the Care of Souls*. Harper & Row 1977.

Williams, H. A., *True Resurrection*. Mitchell Beazley 1972.

Winter, Derek, ed., *Putting Theology to Work*. CFWM 1980.

Wright, Frank, *The Pastoral Nature of the Ministry*. SCM Press 1980.

Index